ISD

From the Ground Up

A No-Nonsense Approach to Instructional Design

Linking People,
Learning & Performance

Chuck Hodell

Ordering information: Books published by ASTD can be ordered by calling 800.628.2783 or 703.683.8100, or via the Website at www.astd.org.

Library of Congress Catalog Card Number: 00-107113

ISBN: 1-56286-143-3

Table of Contents

CONTENTS

Preface

Need for This Book

Trainers need an arsenal of tools at their disposal. Despite the growing use of Web-based training, more than 77 percent of all training is still instructor led (Bassi and Van Buren, 1999). Every year the United States spends more than $30 billion in traditional training environments, according to the American Society for Training & Development (ASTD) (Bassi and Van Buren, 1999). This amount covers the cost of facilitators, materials, and methods that have an excellent track record for success.

ASTD also reports that employee-to-trainer ratios are rising, with more than 700-to-1 ratios in some organizations (Bassi and Van Buren, 1999). That means for every trainer there are more than 700 employees to be trained.

With these heavy demands on their professional skills, trainers are looking for smarter, quicker, and easier ways to perform their design tasks. That is what this book is about—making instructional design smarter, quicker, and easier. It doesn't require magic—just a set of skills that belong in a designer's tool kit.

ISD From the Ground Up is a tool to help bring those skills into the workplace. It provides those beginning their instructional design careers with the basics through a hands-on exercise approach. Experienced instructional designers will find that this book is an effective way to review their skills and practice their techniques in training design.

Acknowledgments

I wish to express my appreciation to Dr. J. Marvin Cook, the man who planted the ISD bug in me; to the folks at ASTD, especially Mark Morrow for his partnership with me on this effort, Cat Russo, and Phil Anderson; to all of my colleagues at the National Labor College including President Susan Schurman and the EDU crew: Jean Dearden, Julie Ann Mendez, Nalini Roy, Lydia Clemons, Isaac Wilson, Cindy Cooke, Brian Gustine, John Amman, and Christa Dicky; to my brothers and sisters in the labor movement who have inspired me to get an education and work in their behalf; to my colleagues at the University of Maryland Baltimore County (UMBC), including Zane Berge and Marie de Verneil, who wrote the excellent chapter on Web-based training, as well as Deb Schreiber, Lin Muilenburg, Colleen Salvatore, Donna Taylor, Kathleen Stitely, Amy Hutchison, and Tim Fitzsimmons; to my graduate students at UMBC who assisted me with this book, including Donna Kinerney, Dawn Kane, Vicky Passion Graff, Amy Rossmark, Bernadette Fortenbaugh, Brian J. Reider, Charlotte Leer, Dana Karp, and especially Ginger Butcher. And to all of my students, past and present. Thanks.

Dedication

Yes, kids, Dad was really writing a book. I love you. To Heather, David, Joe, and the extended Hodell family. Thanks for putting up with me while I plugged away at this.

Reference

Bassi, Laurie J., and Mark E. Van Buren. (1999). *The ASTD State of the Industry Report.* Alexandria, VA: ASTD.

Chuck Hodell
Silver Spring, Maryland
November 2000

Introduction

A Mentor for Instructional Designers

Two instructional designers are sitting at their desks preparing training courses. One is frustrated and struggling hopelessly to design a curriculum, while the other is listening through headphones to a portable stereo and putting the finishing touches on a great training project. A number of things may account for the designers' very different approaches. The biggest difference, however, is the reservoir of instructional design skills that the music lover has acquired.

Every instructional designer has started in the same place in this field—at the beginning. Some learn the hard way through trial and error, whereas others have the advantage of being mentored by a veteran designer. This book provides the benefits of a mentor and puts them readily at hand—whether on your desk or in your briefcase.

You may not even consider yourself an instructional designer. If you are a facilitator, trainer, or classroom teacher, you may look at instructional design as something you have little control over. Many courses or classes are prepared, ready for you to put to use. Eventually, as you gain more experience and others want to take advantage of your talents, you will probably design your own courses or prepare courses for others. It is also possible that an organization will want to use your course for implementation in more than one place at a time, for example in several schools or organizational settings.

Designer's Tool Kit

This book gives you the chance to design now by participating as you read. Chapter exercises give you a chance to practice assembling components of the two major building blocks of instructional design: a design plan and a lesson plan. A **design plan** is the blueprint for a training project and includes all the

1

basic elements of instructional design including behavioral objectives, evaluation tasks, prerequisites for both learners and facilitators, and other essential components you will be introduced to later in the book. The **lesson plan** is the delivery system that takes the design plan and presents it to the end user of the training, the learner.

The skills you will learn or improve upon include:

- analyzing systems, both general and instructional
- defining and working with the generic, or ADDIE (analysis, design, development, implementation, and evaluation) model of instructional design
- performing various analysis operations including population and task analysis and designing and implementing focus groups sessions
- writing objectives and evaluation tasks, and performing other design-phase tasks
- constructing design plans and lesson plans
- performing skills related to the development phase including pilot testing and materials development
- implementing designers' tools
- writing and implementing various evaluation strategies, including Kirkpatrick's four levels of evaluation
- using skills related to Web-based training.

Instructional design isn't any more difficult to learn and put to use than any other process. Yet, a gap exists between the great and the marginal designs in the real world. There are as many different ways to design a new employee orientation as there are new employees. Yet, very few orientations actually make a new employee feel as if he or she made the right decision in picking a new employer. The difference between the great and the marginal is often in the use of instructional systems development to design training. The use of a system to design and implement the program pays dividends in the way a training "feels" to the participants and the benefits it offers an organization.

Instructional systems development (ISD) is a systems approach to training. You may hear it called *instructional development, instructional systems design, systems approach to training*, or several other terms. They all refer to similar approaches to designing curriculum.

The designer's tool kit consists of a variety of instructional design tools for use one at a time or in combination to form a battery of skills to address one or a hundred design challenges.

You will find while working your way through this book that ISD is really nothing more than common sense with a plan. One way to look at planning is to consider an ambitious project, like the building of the Egyptian pyramids. Most of us would agree that it would be important to have a good plan for erecting large granite objects like those. Yet, after more than 4,000 years, no one has been able to satisfactorily explain how thousands of stone rectangles became the pyramids.

Successful training projects look to nondesigners somewhat like pyramids look to most of us. From the outside it appears that designing a curriculum must be a straightforward process. So and so does such and such, and the job gets done. Yet, below the surface a number of design skills and processes combine to form a project of mythical proportions. New employee orientation becomes the organizational equivalent to the pyramids; something that stands the test of time.

What Skills Are Required

A number of specialized skills must be present in an instructional designer's tool kit. Read through the list of instructional design skills in table 1 and determine if you have each skill. This is not a test. It only serves as a snapshot of where you begin the process of building your tool kit. For right now, check "yes" or "no" to the question posed in the table. This inventory will also appear in chapter 12, when you will have an opportunity to compare your beginning skills with your ending skills.

Building Your Design Skills

Readers have the luxury of using this book in several ways, depending on their needs. Whether they are working on a design project or need to brush up on a specific aspect of instructional design, they can consult the chapters that fit their needs. If they are just starting out in the field and are not working on a specific project, they can get an in-depth look at the steps in an instructional project.

The book follows one instructional design project—construction of a poison prevention course—from start to finish so readers can see how it is done. That project appears in the exercise sections that follow chapters 1 through 8. The subject matter is not intended for actual implementation, but to illustrate the instructional design process. After reading each description of the poison prevention project, readers may return to it, substituting a project they are

Table 1. Skills inventory.

Do You Know How to:	Yes	No
Conduct a population analysis		
Design and implement a focus group session		
Write four-part objectives		
Name the four objective domains		
Define and provide examples of at least three instructional methods		
Define and provide examples of at least three distribution methods		
Write at least two evaluation tasks		
Explain the performance agreement principle using an example		
Design evaluations for each of the four Kirkpatrick levels		
Complete a design plan		
Construct a lesson plan		

working on or any other subject matter they choose. The poison prevention material is intended to serve as a place holder for readers' own content.

Readers also have the option of using the design plan in chapter 8 and the lesson plans in chapter 9 and the appendix as templates for their own projects. They have the luxury of picking and choosing the elements of each chapter that fit their needs.

Who Needs This Book

This book is a practitioner's guide to ISD and is grounded in more reality than that in scores of other textbooks. Readers who are still building their ISD skills will find this book a useful and practical guide, without a lot of academic theory. Seasoned practitioners will find it an excellent in-service resource for their own effort at ISD.

Both groups of readers will find that this book provides the basics of great instructional practice as well as practical ways to apply the principles.

Chapters 1 through 10 conclude with exercises that enable readers to gain experience applying the ISD concepts. As they work through each exercise, readers will gain confidence in their use of the concept and find ways to put them to work.

The book is useful for designers at both small and large organizations. One of the biggest myths about instructional design is that it is really only useful when integrated in a large organization. Nothing could be further from the truth. In fact, the largest gains in efficiency and participant success are usually in environments that are either strapped for resources, such as nonprofits and community groups, or in one-person operations, such as classroom teachers or small training organizations. This is true for several reasons not the least of which is that even small moves toward efficiency in small organizations reap great advantages.

A comparison to the stock market will make this clear. Stocks that have low values can gain a few points and show incredible percentage gains, whereas high-valued stocks have to move a great deal to show the same percentage gains in the market. This is why penny stocks are so much fun to buy. You can buy 10,000 shares of a stock for $10 that increases 100 percent in value and walk away with $10 profit. Ten dollars won't even buy you most other stocks on the exchanges. It is the same concept for implementing instructional systems. Small organizations and individuals can experience incredible increases in performance. It is all a matter of context.

A note of warning about any completed instructional design: Review is an essential part of all instructional design, even the best instructional design, even one that is completed using this book. As with any creative process, time may change one's perspective on it. The design that seemed perfect two days before may suddenly appear seriously flawed. This is one advantage of a systems approach to instructional design, since evaluation is a key component of the process. Even a short period of time will yield improvements when evaluation is conducted with an objective eye. It is the ISD equivalent of counting to 10 when someone's upset and wants to speak his or her mind. Evaluation provides time for reflection and reconsideration.

Accumulation of Advantages

If you play chess, you have probably heard the term **accumulation of advantages.** To a chess master, it means that a player has to do a number of individual steps correctly in order to win a match. Most great chess players are thinking many moves ahead in order to chart out a strategy and prepare a defense for any move an opponent might make.

In ISD, accumulation of advantages is about making sure a designer makes all the right moves when designing curriculum. For example, it is impossible to have a great project if a designer leaves out analysis or evaluation. A designer needs to be three steps ahead of any problems in implementing a project and providing solutions when they do arise. For the chess player or the instructional designer, accumulation of advantages is a concept that means winning. And a designer always wants a winning project.

How This Book Is Arranged

This book is a hands-on approach to ISD, not an academic look at the subject. This book has four sections designed to help readers build or enhance their skills as instructional designers. Generally, readers will find the basics in sections 1 and 2, practice in section 3, and additional skills-enhancement materials in section 4. Following is an overview of what readers will find in each section:

Section 1, "The Basics of ISD," contains the basics of instructional systems development. It sets the foundation for the remainder of readers' travels through the book as they visit systems and learn why an instructional system is so integral to success as an instructional designer. The poison prevention project begins here.

Section 2, "Working Through the ADDIE Model," is the nucleus of ISD as readers explore analysis, design, development, implementation, and evaluation in greater detail. They will explore various designer tools, including focus groups, writing objectives, designing evaluation instruments, and many other important aspects of ISD.

Section 3, "The Basics of the Design and Lesson Plans," provides readers with both a design plan and lesson plan, which serve as both learning tools and job aids. Readers can use these tools to assemble their own projects or just use the model as a point of reference. The poison prevention project takes final form here.

Section 4, "Tips for Success," covers skills enhancement and looks to the future. Readers will find an informative, cutting-edge discussion of the ISD practices related to distance education.

The chapters in each section relate to specific themes in instructional design. The arrangement of each topic allows readers to quickly analyze their needs in a specific design area and move where they need to be. To facilitate this time saver, chapters 1 through 10 begin with a statement of what readers should be able to do after completing it.

The book also includes an appendix that illustrates a completed lesson plan for the poison prevention course, Poison Prevention in the Home.

It concludes with a list of resources that provides Web addresses to academic institutions and other sites that offer a wealth of information on practical applications and theory. Readers who want further information on ISD should consult these sites.

Learn and enjoy!

Section 1

THE BASICS OF ISD

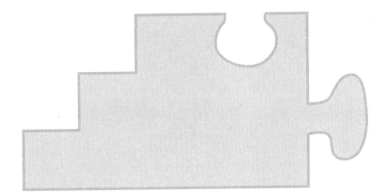

1

Instructional Systems and the ADDIE Model

Chapter Objectives

At the conclusion of this chapter, you should be able to:

- define an instructional system
- define the ADDIE model of ISD
- list advantages and disadvantages of instructional systems.

Instructional Systems

From the perspective of an instructional designer, any undertaking that includes a learner, and the subject matter necessary to learn, requires an instructional system. Instructional designers need inputs like subject matter and resources, a process like ISD, and outputs like curriculum and materials to build a training course. This combination of elements is called an *instructional system*. (See the list of key definitions.)

Key Definitions

- An **instructional system** is an organized and arranged collection of instructional resources that when combined achieve the goal of addressing and providing appropriate training solutions.
- An **extended instructional system** is any and all elements external to the instructional system that have the potential to have an impact on the design process.

(continued on next page)

> ## Key Definitions *(continued)*
>
> - A **project** is a single design effort using an instructional system's approach.
> - The three forms of projects are as follows:
>   - **Singular:** one designer working alone to complete a project.
>   - **Multiple:** more than one designer usually operating within a single departmental or organizational unit.
>   - **Matrixed:** a combination of designers working with other organizational units.
>
> This book describes a system that has five elements: analysis, design, development, implementation, and evaluation. This model is commonly referred to as the **ADDIE model,** after the first letter of each word.

ADDIE Model

The ADDIE model or some derivative of it provides designers with the necessary structure for designing any curriculum, regardless of the instructional methods employed. Anything from lecture to Web-based training starts from the same fundamentals—the ADDIE model.

In the ADDIE model, analysis is the **input** for the system; design, development, and evaluation are the **process;** and implementation is the **output.** These elements overlap somewhat, depending on the project, and because the system is dynamic, there will be some sharing of duties. This book will examine in depth each of the five elements of the ADDIE model, but for now here are some brief descriptions of each one.

Analysis

Analysis is the data-gathering element of instructional design. Here instructional designers assemble all the information they can possibly gather about the project before they consider anything else. Decisions about every aspect of the project must eventually be made. The information that instructional designers gather at this stage will be put to use throughout the system, so it is necessary that they have every scrap of data to ensure the design will be successful.

Design

Design is the blueprinting stage of instructional systems during which instructional designers create the blueprint for a project with all the specifications necessary to complete the project. During this stage, instructional designers write the objectives, construct course content, and complete the design plan.

Development

Materials production and pilot testing are the hallmarks of development. At this stage, most nondesigners begin to see progress. Everything from lecture notes to virtual reality is brought from design to deliverable. Before instructional designers move from development to implementation, it is wise for them to do pilot testing to ensure that deliverables do not have to be redeveloped. Because of the time and expense involved, no one wants to reprint manuals or recode a technology-based project after a project goes into implementation. The pilot testing process allows organizations to implement any necessary changes in the project before the expenses associated with materials development are realized. The time and effort expended in pilot testing is well worth the effort, if for this reason alone. Pilot testing also helps designers feel confident that what they have designed works.

Implementation

The most familiar of the elements is implementation. At implementation, the design plan meets the learner, and the content is delivered. The evaluation process that most designers and learners are familiar with takes place in this element. Evaluation is used to gauge the degree to which learners meet objectives and facilitators or technologies deliver the project.

Evaluation

Evaluation doesn't deserve to be listed last in the ADDIE model because it takes place in every element and surrounds the instructional design process. Evaluation is a constant guard at the gate of failure.

The advantages of using an instructional system are numerous, the most important being the ability to design projects quickly and efficiently. Nothing is left to chance or ignored when a designer stays within the framework of the ADDIE or other ISD models. One possible disadvantage is the necessity of a designer to be familiar with the ISD process.

The ADDIE Model at Work

The ADDIE model is best put to use as soon as someone in an organization thinks there is a need for a training course. A description of the way an employee at one company applied the ADDIE model follows. The company, which requested anonymity, provides information-technology to manage food and beverage operations at ballparks, stadiums, arenas, casinos, and other establishments in the hospitality industry. Brian J. Reider, the instructional designer, was considering creating a course for installers, support technicians, dealer representatives, and hardware technicians. The course would provide these staff members with the information they needed to provide the best possible help to their customers.

Following are the steps Reider followed as he applied the ADDIE model to creation of a course.

Problem

Reider defined the problem as whether to create a course as a way to allow the company to continue providing the best support for the customer. One consideration he noted was that he was not an expert on hardware.

Analysis

During this data-gathering stage, Reider tried to get answers to the following questions:

- Why do we need this course?
- What makes this hardware so different from the other that it needs its own course?
- What information needs to be covered in the course?

He used face-to-face interviews to gather information that would be relevant in the course. He interviewed support technicians (software and hardware), installation technicians, hardware technical writers, members of the hardware research and development department, and the director of Hardware Services to help determine what information is necessary for a technician in the field. He also read support cases to see what some of the major problem areas were.

He concluded that the following topics should be included in the course:

- how this software and hardware are different from others
- basic knowledge of all components (Parts Identification)
- what parts are replaceable

- how to install the replacement parts
- how to convert one model to the newer model
- how to use some basic troubleshooting techniques.

Design

In this blueprinting stage of instructional design, Reider created observable and measurable terminal objectives for the course. The design took into account the need to create an evaluation later in the development. Reider had the subject matter experts review the objectives and give any feedback. From the objectives, he determined that the best delivery method for instruction would be an instructor-led course with extensive hands-on exercises.

He created an organizational chart (similar to a course or topic map) so that he had a graphical representation of the topics and subtopics to be discussed. This helped him group and link different topics to one another. It also allowed him to create the necessary enabling objectives.

Development

Materials production and pilot testing are the key elements of this stage. For developing the course, Reider followed the nine events of instruction, which Gagne developed as a sequence for lesson plan design. (A description of the nine events of instruction appears in chapter 4.) Reider also maintained contact with some subject matter experts to ensure that the material he was creating was accurate.

Reider was becoming increasingly knowledgeable about the hardware and was actually able to identify, remove, and replace all of the replaceable parts. While it was disassembled, he and other staff members used a digital camera to photograph the different components. They will use these photographs for a parts identification job aid on the company's Website.

Reider did not create a formal evaluation for the course due to the constraints on the length of the course and the purpose of the course.

Implementation

The course was implemented soon thereafter.

Evaluation

Before the formal implementation of the course, a pilot class was held. The participants of the pilot class were new hires and members of the training department. The participants had no knowledge of the hardware. At the end of the pilot class, a focus group was held to obtain feedback on the course. The participants completed a level one evaluation form. Revision to the course was made on the basis of responses from the focus group, responses on a level one course evaluation, and the feedback from the instructor.

Reider reported that he made minimal changes as a result of the level one evaluation and the focus group. The course received great reviews, and the students enjoyed all the hands-on activity. Reider taught the course at various company offices throughout the United States as well as to company employees in Germany and Hong Kong.

Other ISD Models

There are probably as many ISD models as there are instructional designers. Although other formal models exist for us to follow and learn from, each individual designer does things a little bit differently in the real world. No two projects work the same way, and there have never been two instructional designers that design projects exactly the same way. In fact, not every instructional designer uses the ADDIE model, but the five elements of analysis, design, development, implementation, and evaluation should always be present in ISD.

As an instructional designer gains experience, the ISD elements combine in a way that works for them. Derivations of the model will be necessary to meet different design strategies. Different designers write objectives differently, and no two surveys ever look exactly the same. Every designer eventually evolves to create a unique model of ISD based on the same basic ADDIE structure. It is not uncommon in some ISD models to see an additional level of analysis or evaluation or another element added to meet a specific design or organizational need. It is safe to say there are as many ISD models as there are designers.

The cardinal rule of ISD is to never leave out analysis and evaluation, the two most commonly avoided and abused elements of the model. Projects without analysis and evaluation can be quickly spotted by two qualities: they seldom work and no one ever really knows why they failed.

Characteristics of a Well-Designed Program

The saying that hard work is usually disguised as luck has great resonance in training. The most successful training programs have the appearance of being effortlessly designed and delivered. The content is appropriate for the audience, there is just enough material to cover the time allowed, participants are able to meet the objectives, and evaluations assure that the course design provides the desired results.

At the other extreme, a program that was put together with little planning or little thought about the desired results leaves learners confused, and the evaluations, if there are any, concentrate on nontraining issues like the comfort of the chairs or the cleanliness of the restrooms. Participants leave those programs wondering why they bothered to invest their time. The difference between these two situations is typically directly related to the time and expertise invested in the instructional design process.

The evidence that a program has been well designed is the participants in the training. They have learned.

Putting What You Have Learned Into Action

Now, let's work through some exercises to build your confidence and start you on the road to designing a course of your own.

Exercise 1.1. Poison prevention course, part 1. The instructional design system.

This is the first exercise in the poison prevention project. These exercises, which appear in chapters 1 through 9, illustrate the ISD concepts presented in this book. Exercise 1.1 shows the system surrounding the poison prevention project. Just as in any training program, inputs and outputs are joined by process elements to design a curriculum. This design process takes place after analysis and provides a designer with the framework necessary to build a project. Let's examine this system using the information provided in analysis and its elements.

- **Inputs:** community's need to reduce incidents of poisoning, community's access to volunteers, people who have expressed an interest in taking a course, small amount of money, places to hold training sessions, community's access to data and materials related to poison prevention, and great instructional designer.

(continued on next page)

Exercise 1.1. Poison prevention course, part 1.
The instructional design system. *(continued)*

- **Process elements:** gathering poison prevention data and materials, developing a project design plan, developing a project lesson plan, designing evaluation instruments, training volunteers, and printing materials.
- **Outputs:** training course and materials, training programs implemented at local community centers, reduction in poisoning cases in the year following the beginning of the training.

Exercise 1.2. The instructional design system.

Now consider a course you are working on. What are the inputs, process elements, and outputs for that project?

1. **Inputs:** _____

_____

_____

_____

2. **Process elements:** _____

_____

_____

_____

3. **Outputs:** _____

_____

_____

_____

Section 2

WORKING THROUGH THE ADDIE MODEL

2
Analysis

Chapter Objectives

At the conclusion of this chapter, you should be able to:

- determine the difference between training and nontraining problems
- list three data-gathering steps
- describe two basic components of a focus group and two ground rules for a focus group
- list the four levels of detail in task analysis
- describe three critical elements of a population analysis
- list at least three instructional methods and their uses.

A Cumulative Approach

The notion of starting with nothing and finishing with something has a great deal of appeal to most of us. Turning a pile of lumber into a house or 10 yards of fabric into curtains demonstrates creativity and manifests a sense of accomplishment. But these efforts don't start from nothing. You cannot build a house or sew curtains unless you start with some raw materials and have enough information to successfully complete the project.

Isaac Newton has long been quoted as saying that his incredible accomplishments in physics were just the result of his "...standing on the shoulders of giants...." The wisdom and modesty reflected in that statement aside, what Newton was alluding to was the cumulative effect of individual discoveries gathered together. Designers do well to identify with the simple truth of this concept: Gather all the data you can, determine how they fit together, and then design something more powerful than each of the single elements alone.

Chess masters and other players know that there isn't a single move that can win the game without another move before it that clears the way. World-class players actually think many moves ahead in order to place the pieces exactly where they need them to capture the game. This concept is exactly the process that excellent designers use to design a project. One careful move follows another until the project is completed. Designers must think several moves ahead in order to clear the way for the ADDIE elements to follow. If they skip just one move, they have placed their project in jeopardy.

Instructional designers would be well served to adapt the mythical curiosity of the cat and a Sherlock Holmesian eagerness to uncover even the most illusive bits of information. This sense of discovery is at the heart of every good designer.

Analysis Basics

In the analysis stage, instructional designers can never know too much. Curiosity is the first analysis skill that belongs in their tool kit, where it will pay many dividends.

Seven key questions require answers during analysis. By addressing each of these questions, instructional designers ensure that they gather all the data they are likely to need as they work their way through the ADDIE system. The questions also help designers check that they have focused on all the possible aspects of the course under consideration. In short, these questions serve as a reality check:

- What is the need?
- What is the root cause?
- What are the goals of the training?
- What information is needed, and how is it gathered?
- How will the training be structured and organized?
- How will the training be delivered?
- When should training be revised?

The rest of the chapter describes each of these questions as well as some common problems that instructional designers face.

What Is the Need?

Need is the gatekeeper for entry into analysis. If there is no need for the course, there is no need to perform an analysis. This relationship between need and analysis holds true even if a designer has been given an assignment to design a course and has no option except completing it with only two weeks' notice.

Many designers believe that training is the best solution to numerous problems in an organization. Experience shows, however, that some problems do not require training solutions. In fact, they are not training problems at all. For example, the staff at a company may not be communicating with one another. Although they send messages by intranet, the messages are lost in cyberspace and do not reach the intended people. Training will not help those employees improve their communications because the problem is that they need an upgraded intranet system.

A range of issues exists that cannot be fixed with training. Other examples include low wages, miserable working conditions, and the lack of proper equipment. Undoubtedly, there are solutions for these issues, and performance improvement specialists can find ways to solve them. An instructional designer's role in an unhappy work situation would not include designing a course called Being Happy With Your Terrible Salary.

Designers must determine early on if a training intervention can remedy anything about an apparent problem. If they determine that a training solution is possible, they can move on to the next level of analysis. If they determine that training is not the solution, then they must recognize the reality and move to find other solutions.

The cardinal rule of the analysis element of ISD is, Make sure there is a training solution before providing one.

Not every need requires training. In the larger world of performance improvement, nontraining solutions are viable and can have a sizable impact. However, within instructional design, the gatekeeper function is critical regardless of the eventual solution. That function enables the designer to get the information needed to make an informed decision.

Typically, designers find that the type of training selected as a solution is based on a learner's lack of knowledge, skills, or abilities, or a combination of these elements. Training solutions are nearly always available for any performance need that falls within this group. Training does not offer solutions for wages, benefits, working conditions, organizational procedures, or personality conflicts.

What Is the Root Cause?

The first task for a designer is to identify the need and determine the root cause of any problems that may exist. Sometimes the need and root cause are relatively easy to uncover. At other times, they may take some digging to reveal. Designers must listen carefully to what they hear and use their logic filter to test each potential issue.

It is important to point out that even though a need appears to be instructional in nature, it might not be. That assessment might be made on the basis of symptoms and not the root cause of the problem. Just as in medicine, treating the symptoms may initially reduce the pain, but it seldom cures the illness.

Following are two situations in which training is not the solution:

- An office is displaying symptoms of discord that are interfering with normal work activities. After some analysis, it is determined that a new supervisor is not working out well with the group. Rather than dealing with the supervisor, management suggests that the training department offer some courses on attitude readjustment and team building. This intervention will not solve the problem because it does not touch the root cause—the supervisor.

- At another organization, an undercurrent of sexual harassment problems gained the attention of the executive director. Management expected violations within the organization to diminish or even disappear as a result of training, but following the training, reports of violations soared and management blamed the training for the increase. The unexpected result of the training was the empowerment of workers who had experienced problems and now felt obligated to come forward with complaints. The root problem, though, was several individuals who did not see themselves as doing anything offensive.

Here are two situations in which training may be solutions:

- The partners at a law firm are upset about the sudden decline in the quality and quantity of their support staff's work. A senior partner investigates and learns that the office manager has switched word-processing programs. The new software is designed specifically for law offices and requires the staff to learn new commands. The office manager chose not to accept the initial training, which the supplier offered at a reduced rate at the time of purchase. The solution now is simple: to give software training to the staff. Unfortunately, the cost for training will be higher than if it had been ordered earlier. The firm is also paying a high cost in the diminished morale.

- A small nonprofit group has a yearly fund-raising drive to support its community-based programs. This year the group decided to move from door-to-door solicitation to phone solicitation. Donations are off by more than 30 percent, and the board of directors is livid. The executive director has followed the advice of a consulting firm that has assisted a number of for-profit organizations to improve their sales. Unfortunately, the nonprofit group tried to save money by using older volunteers who had trouble reading the calling scripts that were printed in small type. Several approaches may solve this difficulty. A role-playing training class for the volunteers might help them perfect their calls. Another solution might be to enlarge the type on the volunteer's calling sheets.

What Are the Goals of the Training?

Anyone who is going to design a training project must know the rationale for the project. The rationale is a mission statement that clearly states the project's reason for existing. It is the heart and soul of the work to be done. The place to start is with the sponsoring department, manager, organization, or client, who can communicate the goals to the designer. Designers need to verify or correct assumptions that may exist. It is important to ask questions like, What does success for this project mean to you? and When will you be happy with this project? The aim is to get to the bottom of the motivational issues because things that may seem trivial to the designer may be a major issue in a project. With projects for internal clients, designers should be sure the results match the unit's goals as well as the goals of the larger organization. By attending to both groups, designers will protect themselves from getting caught in the crossfire if the project does not resonate with the larger organizational goals.

Sometimes the goals of the sponsor and the reality of the content do not make sense, and the designer must step back and find out why. For example, it is not uncommon for an organization to want to use a new technology for training in an effort to look current with the trends in a certain industry, although analysis may show that the learners do not need or want a technology-based solution. In this case, the goals of the organization and the reality of the situation do not match. On those occasions, someone may be operating under a hidden and self-interested agenda. Instructional designers must be alert to the possibility that they may discover problems like these in the populations they serve:

- Career boosting is usually framed by someone whose real interest is in showcasing his or her contribution to management. Evidence that career boosting is at work on a project is often in design that is heavy on production values and low on instructional design values. Training designed for show can often backfire when the cost to produce unnecessary or ineffective training is discovered.

- Getting-even training is discovered when the training goals seem to be, "We'll show them how to . . ." or "They won't do that to us again."
- Propaganda training is always designed to send a message to someone. Evidence is that the message is more important than the behavioral objective.

Sound goals designers are likely to see might include an increase of sales by a certain percentage or reduction in the number of mistakes being generated by the implementation of a new software package in an organization.

What Information Is Needed, and How Is It Gathered?

The first three questions helped instructional designers determine that training can address the need and is consistent with individual and organizational goals. Now it is necessary to obtain information in both subject matter and nonsubject matter areas.

Subject matter is the heart of the project, and nonsubject matter is the soul. The information on both will form the basis for the design plan. This book will look at design plans in much more detail in the next chapter.

The nonsubject matter information needed for the design plan includes the rationale for the course, described under "What Are the Goals for the Training," population data, course structure, and deliverables. The subject matter information will eventually end up as objectives, evaluation strategies, facilitator prerequisites, and learner prerequisites.

Building a Population Profile

One of the basic tenets of politics is always know the players. A politician would never consider making a move without checking to see how a population of voters felt about a particular issue. A politician would know the demographics including age, income, party affiliation, gender, ethnicity, and any other variable that could have an impact on his or her success in the next election. Trainers need to know the players just as much as a politician. In fact, a trainer's chance at success is just as perilous as a politician's.

A population analysis provides trainers with the information they need to ensure that they communicate in a way their audience will understand. A software training program should not include computer jargon, for example, if the audience is not computer literate.

The first step in identifying the population is to develop a list of all possible factors that could have an impact on designers' thinking and ultimately on their success. Recently, for a project in a Middle Eastern country, it was important to honor differences that would not normally be an issue in Western countries. Some of the factors designers had to consider included:

- **Education levels:** Literacy was a concern.
- **Religious influence:** It was necessary that designers honor prayer times and other religious ceremonies that might occur during training hours.
- **Gender interaction:** Traditional gender roles created challenges in designing group activities including role-play exercises.
- **Attendance issues:** In many Middle Eastern countries, participants do not honor starting and stopping times as rigidly as they do in the United States.
- **Evaluation techniques:** Some populations are hesitant to offer criticism of one another or to question a facilitator.
- **Appropriate materials:** Designers must consider participants' views about how materials represent them, especially graphic representations. The manner of dress and types of activities shown in materials must be acceptable to the target population.
- **Religious schedules:** In many areas of the world, the normal workday is Sunday to Thursday. Variables of this occur within individual countries and religious groups represented in a typical population of learners. It is also important not to schedule training during religious holidays that are not familiar to Westerners.

Ultimately this list led to a comprehensive training project that reflected the needs of the population and helped ensure a good start to the design plan. It is important that all the elements in a population study have an effect on the design.

The first step in conducting a population analysis is to establish which of the issues may influence the project's success. A simple matrix, like the one in table 2, works fine for this step. For each element that may have an effect, the designer will say whether or not it could affect the outcome of the project, why, and whether he or she can do anything about it. The row "age" shows how someone might complete this table for a course on use of the Internet at a senior citizen home.

Table 2. Population analysis.

Issue	Influence Success? Yes or No	Why?	What Can I Do?
Age	Yes	Seniors may not have experience using computers, let alone the Internet.	Split the class into two groups—those with computer experience and those without.
Culture			
Education level			
Ethnicity			
Gender			
Incentive			
Language skill			
Motivation			

The designer should analyze each of these issues with one question in mind: "Can this element affect the outcome of this project?" For each element, the designer would ask if it has the potential to cause success or failure. Motivation and incentive issues alone can sink a really well-designed training project if they have not been taken into account. If the answer is yes, it can cause success or failure, the designer must address why and then what he or she is going to do about it.

Designing and Conducting a Focus Group

Every instructional designer should be familiar with focus groups and the value they bring to analysis and evaluation. Focus groups range from informal conversations to videotaped productions, and there are almost as many styles as there are designers to facilitate them. The term **focus group** derives from the intent of this analysis tool, which is to focus on a particular topic and capture participants' comments.

Focus groups are used widely for gauging participants' views on such diverse topics as a political issue or a new product being brought to market. An instructional designer might be interested in using this tool to determine a population's attitudes about a proposed training strategy or to uncover issues that cause problems in a work group.

Regardless of the content or style of a focus group, its single most important component is the facilitator. Each focus group requires a facilitator who remains comfortable if tensions arise (as they surely do) when participants express strong opinions and who is responsible enough to maintain control. It is painful to see an inexperienced facilitator buckle under the pressure of two or more opinionated participants who take over the process.

The model presented here represents the author's experience with these groups in a training setting. Designers will undoubtedly evolve their own strategies and even change them as conditions warrant.

In general, focus groups tend to be useful in data-gathering situations that involve emotions, human interactions, and attitudes. They are also a very powerful problem-solving tool.

Every focus group should have at least four basic components: ground rules, warm-up questions, focus questions, and closers. Following is a description of each.

- **Ground rules:** Ground rules set the code of conduct for the group, both in terms of topic and process. Ground rules should be clearly stated and should appear on an easel sheet or in any other visible place. Common ground rules governing process include time limits on the length of the focus group activity and time limits on individual comments.

  Topic boundaries include facilitator privilege, such as the authority to moderate as necessary, and confidentiality and nonconfidentiality statements.

  Time limits are an absolute necessity for most focus groups, although it is sometimes tricky to gauge the time needed to collect data. Time limits assist in focusing participants' thoughts on the topic and help enforce participant and topic boundaries. Typical phrases to use to move the discussion along are

  — "I'm sorry we must move on or we will run out of time."

  — "It sounds like we've hit on a hot topic. We could go on indefinitely, but we have a lot on our plate today; for now we need to move on so that we can meet our session objectives."

Individual comments should be limited to 90 seconds or less. Longer comments become speeches, and if one participant is perceived as being in control, others may feel stifled or unimportant. It is sometimes useful to ask participants to think and respond as if they were writing bulleted comments on the topic.

If focus groups are to be a success, it is vitally important to set topic boundaries and enforce them. Facilitators must limit the questions to one or a few topics and let participants know they will be cut off it they wander from them. A focus group concerning workload, for example, can quickly turn into a history of the industrial age. It usually only takes one corrective maneuver to keep that from happening.

Facilitator privilege is the right to control the focus group process. The facilitator is the traffic cop of the focus group. There can be no compromise on this component or the facilitator may quickly lose control of the group .

Confidentiality must also be addressed. The decision to record, transcribe, or otherwise document the group's actions will have an effect on the outcome. Some participants may want comments on record to substantiate a particular view about the topic, whereas others will not feel comfortable saying anything of value if it will be attributed to them. Designers need to discuss these perspectives with a client to eliminate any misunderstanding before the session is held. No matter which choice designers make, they must inform the participants.

- **Warm-up questions:** Facilitators usually use warm-up questions to get a group talking and thinking. Some designers call these **framing questions** because they open the gate for participants to enter and frame the rest of the process.

  Venting is a key element of this early stage of the focus group. Hidden agendas and bottled-up frustrations come to the surface and must be vented or they could damage the focus group. Thirty seconds of griping at this early stage is seldom a problem. Thirty seconds later may negate the entire session.

  If a focus group is considering members' attitudes about a new process or procedure, a warm-up question might ask them about their feelings toward change in general. For example, for a focus group about workplace change, the warm-up question might be, "How are things going in the office right now?" or "What is the hot topic of discussion right now?" These warm-up questions start to frame the context of the issue. Immediately the participants know the general direction in which the facilitator is heading. If the participants express tension, anxiety, or anger at this point, the facilitator at least has a barometer of the level of emotion that the topic is generating. Eventually the facilitator will get to the subject, usually with the pressure removed to a degree that allows for an excellent focus group.

- **Focus questions:** This section is the heart of a focus group. All of the activity before and after supports this group of questions. Designers should first work on these questions as they begin designing their focus groups. Then they can build everything around them.

In a group focusing on workplace change, for example, the designer would be interested in the participants' reaction to proposed or suggested changes. The designer might offer a range of options for the groups' reaction, or the designer might build toward one predefined series of changes that an organization might be considering and gauge the participants' reaction. Either way, the focus questions are the most important of all the questions.

If a company is asking about change because it wants to introduce work in teams, for example, the designer might ask, "How do you feel about working in teams?" or "What do you think of the following types of changes?" These questions are different ways of getting to the main point.

Facilitators will explore the focus questions in more depth as they begin to gauge the reactions and comments. They sometimes find it useful to narrow the scope of the discussion until they find the level of "no further usefulness."

- **Closers:** A successful close requires a smooth transition. A final question allows participants to bring the topic to closure. Facilitators should ask questions that require some thought and let the participants know that they have been listening to what they say. Here are some examples of closers:

  — "If you have the opportunity to say one thing to the boss about this topic, what would it be?" _____

  _____

  — "If you were the boss and could do one thing about this situation, what would it be?" _____

  _____

  — "You have just been put in charge of fixing this situation, what is your first step?" _____

  _____

All of these include elements of ownership, leadership, and empowerment.

- **Other focus group issues:** Some of the other important issues include attendance by nonparticipants, location, size, and makeup. Many times people are so interested in the process or consider themselves large enough stakeholders that they demand to be part of the facilitation. This is generally a bad idea, especially if the person sitting in is a stakeholder in the discussion. The presence of a manager or outspoken observer can change the tone of a group. Occasionally, a stakeholder offers input or answers the questions and skews the results of the session entirely.

The location of the focus group process is also important. If a topic is controversial and opinions may end up being polarized, facilitators should move to a neutral site. The home field advantage is really a disadvantage in some situations. For example, a labor-management topic is best handled on a neutral site to avoid the appearance of managerial influence of the group. Facilitators should not be afraid to move to a new venue if the conditions warrant and the budget allows for it. Even a move across the street to a hotel or restaurant can make the difference between getting what they need or making the problem worse. A move might make participants in a labor-management focus group more willing to say what they are thinking, whereas they might supply stock answers or not participate at all if they are at a stakeholder's environment.

It is important that the focus group resemble the population it is analyzing. Fine-tuning the size and makeup can be a challenge. In some groups this is easy because the focus groups are themselves the entire population. In larger populations, facilitators need to determine which variables are important to the content and assemble their participants in a way that represents those interests. For example, if the population for a focus group on the issue of day care in the workplace is not influenced by age, then age should not be a sampling standard. Gender might very well be a sampling condition. Other qualifiers might be job title, seniority, education, and ethnicity; in fact, anything that might engender a difference of opinion could be a qualifier.

Developing Surveys

Every instructional designer uses surveys. How the designers use them can determine success or failure. Here are some of the basics of surveys:

- How questions are asked is the key. Open-ended questions lead to open-ended answers. For **quantifiable data,** designers must ask quantifiable questions and supply specific ranges of answers. For example, a designer who wants to ask 100 workers about their ability to use a specific software package might ask either of these questions:

— How well can you use the software? _____

_____

— How well can you use the software? (a) very well, (b) know most of the commands I need, (c) struggle with some commands, (d) not very much, (e) not at all.

In the first example, the designer will get a range of answers that cannot be easily compared to each other or a standard from which to start designing. The designer who asks the second question will be able to compute percentages and use those data to design the course based on quantifiable data. If 50 percent say they know the software very well and 20 percent say not very much, the designer can eliminate the top 50 percent and concentrate on the bottom 50 percent who need skill enhancement.

- **Rating questions** also are useful to providing insight into content. For example, a designer might ask:
  - How do you rate your ability to perform the following functions using the software: Mail merge (a) flawlessly, (b) few problems, (c) many problems, (d) cannot use it at all.

The designer would then ask about all of the commands or skills that might be considered content in the course. The designer will build the basis of the content for the course as he or she works through the questions. This same process works for almost any skill-based analysis.

- For sampling **attitudes,** designers can also turn to surveys and change the style of questions to some degree. In the case of a workplace in chaos, the questions might be
  - How would you rate the number of interpersonal problems in the office? (a) no problems, (b) some minor problems, (c) many problems, (d) nothing but problems.
  - In your opinion, what is the atmosphere like in the office? (a) no tension, (b) some tension, (c) very tense, (d) chaos.

Using the SME

SME stands for subject matter experts, whom designers like to call shmees. Some instructional designers work with SMEs regularly, whereas others never work with them. The need for SMEs varies with the kind of instructional design.

Working with SMEs is an art in itself. The designer's tool of working effectively with subject matter experts is a valuable one to enhance or develop.

SMEs fall in one of two types of general category. Some have expertise in a specific skill, such as painting or electrical work, and are brought on to a project to provide data for apprenticeship materials, procedural manuals, or another aspect of the project. Many of these SMEs have never done any type of design work before. Designers must be sure that they are clear as to what information they are asking the SMEs to provide, especially those who are new to the design process. Working with objectives and evaluations might be new to them, and it is important that they realize that they only need to provide technical information and that the designer will take care of the rest.

The other kind of SME is more academic, and the project typically is the result of research or experience gained in the field, or both. They are brought to a project to offer expertise in specialized areas. This group is likely to include professionals with advanced degrees and academic standing. Clear lines of demarcation and responsibility are vital. It is also important that the designers in this environment have both the decision-making authority and responsibility for instructional design issues.

One of the most important keys to working with SMEs is clarity. Most are eager to work on instructional design projects and just need to know the rules. Everyone likes to have his or her knowledge and experience recognized and utilized. Working with designers should be a great experience for them and once they realize that the designers are there to provide the instructional framework, they can relax and concentrate on the content.

It is critically important to choose the right SMEs. The following rules are a useful guide to making the selection:

- Only use SMEs with recent (one year or less) experience in the content area. The pace of change in most fields is such that people with recent experience are considered current in the field. Every field of study is different, but most change considerably in a year.

- Ask around and find out which SMEs are considered the best by others in the peer group.

- Interview before deciding to help eliminate possible personality conflicts.

- Determine if the SMEs have the time to devote to the design process.

- Determine how SMEs will be compensated before starting.

- Review and resolve any copyright issues with SMEs before starting.

- If relevant, ask for writing samples or previous content-related materials.
- Determine if any previous instructional design experience exists.

A little time in finding the best SMEs early in the process may eliminate an irrevocable error later during your project.

There are three basic models for the roles of designers in curriculum development:

- The designer is the only person involved and is the subject matter expert.
- The designer has some subject matter knowledge but works with SMEs.
- The designer has little if any subject matter knowledge and relies on SMEs for assistance.

The power of excellent training comes not from subject matter content, but from the ISD process that designs, implements, and evaluates that training. Anyone who doubts the truth of that statement should compare training programs in any field that are designed using ISD and those that are not. The contrast is obvious.

How Will the Training Be Structured and Organized?

The Importance of Task Analysis

Task analysis is the grandparent of all analysis methods. It involves the process of breaking down a job or assignment into each task associated with it to learn the skills and knowledge necessary to perform it. The data gathered in this process assist the designer in building the structure of the project, including instructional methods and media. They also tell how best to organize objectives and evaluations in a logical continuum from beginning to end.

Task analysis is something every instructional designer does and can be used for a variety of situations. Jobs, skills, procedures, processes, and, of course, tasks are usually best analyzed in this manner. Task analysis is the first step for an instructional designer who needs to replicate anything that involves human interaction in a series of steps. An instructional designer would perform a task analysis to be sure a lesson covers every step a person needs to know in order to perform the job, skill, procedure, process, or task.

Even though it is such a fundamental tool of the instructional designer, task analysis is often done poorly or given little preparation time. In fact, it is not as simple as one might assume. Four levels of detail exist in a task analysis: job, task, skill, and subskill (see "Task Analysis Examples").

Task Analysis Examples

Following are examples of task analysis for an air traffic controller and a sales executive.

- **Job:** air traffic controller
  - — **Task:** giving an airplane clearance to land at an airport
  - — **Skills:** monitoring a number of data screens and looking out the window of the tower
  - — **Subskill:** checking the radar screen for possible problems.
- **Job:** vice president of sales
  - — **Task:** monthly reporting
  - — **Skills:** gathering data, writing the report, and so forth
  - — **Subskill:** accessing the organization's spreadsheets and locating the sales figures.

Some instructional designers spend most of their professional life working in situations that require them to follow technical task-analysis procedures. Imagine trying to perform a task analysis on a job like that of manager of an energy-producing nuclear reactor. That job has numerous tasks that must be replicated exactly the way they are engineered because a misstep in the task analysis could put people's lives in jeopardy. Consider what would happen if a task analysis missed a key step in a safety procedure. As a result of that omission, employees might not receive training for a specific problem that might occur. No training probably means diminished effectiveness in dealing with the problem.

Several steps are vitally important in task analysis from the perspective of a designer:

- **Define the target of the analysis:** Whom are you going to work with? What titles or responsibilities do you want to analyze?

- **Choose the methodology:** Will you use task analysis, focus groups, or other methods of analysis?

- **Select the analysis subjects:** Choose the best candidates for analysis. Typically, these are the people who actually do the work and are considered the best at it. It helps to work with several individuals who are struggling with a task so designers can see why they are having trouble.

Task Analysis Field Visit

One of the best ways to learn the art of task analysis is to go into the real world and give it a try. This isn't nearly as difficult as it may seem at first. Designers actually perform task analysis many times a day without thinking about it. A good example might be standing in line to use an unfamiliar automated teller machine. As people work their way up the line, they are actually doing task analysis as they watch those in front operate the machine. Each time one person performs an operation, people in line are observing and remembering how it is done. People in line—those analyzing—note when someone makes a mistake and remember to avoid those same errors.

How Will the Training Be Delivered?

Instructional designers need to determine the distribution methods and instructional methods they will be working with early in their planning, sometimes before really starting the project. It is essential that these two elements be in place before designers get too involved with the design phase.

Possible Instructional Methods

Instructional designers make choices that determine how their learners interact with the subject matter. The designer's tool of matching innovative distribution methods and instructional methods is important.

Instructional methods are techniques that designers use to link objectives with learners. Lectures, group discussions, and case studies all serve as the link between the learner and subject matter, much the same way as a book or Webpage links information with the end user. Distribution methods are the ways designers deliver the instructional methods. Proper matching of distribution and instructional methods and platforms also saves time and energy, both for the designer and the learner.

These are some of the more frequently used instructional methods:

- **Lecture:** With few exceptions, instructional designers should only use lectures in combination with other methods. They might use them alone if they have an inspirational facilitator and want to inspire learners. Otherwise, learners will be fighting back yawns and hunger pains while a facilitator is lecturing. With lectures, it is important to have in place the design elements of clear time limits as well as liberal use of visuals or other stimulators.

- **Role play:** In role plays, learners enact the roles of people placed in various situations in an effort to closely match the training with the real world. Role plays are a great way of placing learners in the action of solving a problem or practicing a skill. Instructional designers must be mindful of any issues that could cause problems if they use role-playing with a group of introverts or a population facing some physical or emotional challenges. Designers must take the time to prepare both the role and scenario descriptions and very precise instructions to both learners and facilitators.

- **Case study:** This method moves the learner up the cognitive ladder and requires decisions, either in a group or singularly. Case studies are great ways to provide instruction in cognitive skills like negotiating, facilitating, reasoning, and constructing solutions. Instructional designers must be careful to ensure that the cases are relevant to their learners. If the cases are out of the learners' contextual framework, they are not likely to hold the learners' interest. It is vitally important that the instructor provides complete case studies, not just bits and pieces of a case. Incomplete information can easily turn a case intended to illustrate a marketing challenge into a case solved by the company giving employees two weeks additional vacation every year. For example, a case study might say that employees were working without any days off, but it might fail to mention that the extra work was because the office was being moved to another building. Without providing complete information, readers may be sympathetic to the workers and want to give them extra vacation.

- **Simulations:** Practice, practice, and more practice. Simulation is one of the best methods for getting learners to practice a skill, process, task, or procedure. It is also great for psychomotor skills. Simulations are the process of performing a task in a safe environment. They are especially helpful for dangerous or expensive tasks. Psychomotor objectives are exercised in simulations because there is no chance of damaging expensive equipment or injuring a participant in a dangerous procedure.

- **Gaming:** Gaming is the process of placing participants in the position of having multiple choices to make in an exercise that borders on real life but provides the safety of a simulation. Just as video games simulate some level of reality, gaming provides the same safe environment without subjecting participants to the dangers of actually performing a task. Some of the best gaming is sophisticated and reaches the limits of technology. Many military applications are right at the corner of reality and surrealism.

- **Critical incident:** This method is used in many training areas that challenge the ability of a learner to react quickly to a problem. Essentially, this is a version of a case study, but it leaves out some of the key data. Airline pilots are subjected to critical incident methods when they simulate flights that develop problems. The extensive use of flight data recorders has allowed the advancement of this method in transportation training.

- **Drill:** Keep doing it, doing it, doing it. Drills are used extensively in computer-based training. For example, many programs require learners to enter words or numbers numerous times to complete a sentence or math problem.

- **Job aid:** This training method pays great dividends in many projects. Job aids are any material that workers keep at hand for easy reference, such as a printed form, cheat sheet, or procedures manual, that contains information on a concept or skill. Since our memory is often unreliable, it is useful to have something in hand that supports the concept or skill involved. Job aids can many times stand on their own and not require any class or technology time to implement.

- **Critique:** This is a modified case study approach that requires determining the strengths and weaknesses of a situation or process, then finding a solution. An annual review by a boss is a valid instructional method.

- **Discussion:** In this context, discussion is directed, follows another activity, and creates the environment for interactivity. The discussions may be large group, small group, buzz groups, or teams. As a general rule, the discussion should not involve groups larger than 25 or 30 learners. If size is an issue, the group should be broken down into workable chunks. It is important that instructional designers prepare both the facilitator and learners before any discussion starts so they know what they will be discussing and why. Without direction or preparation, the group may wander off the subject.

- **In basket:** Learners participate by working through a pile of data sitting in front of them, usually on a desk. They have to make decisions about each item, and the results offer a snapshot of their ability to solve problems. This method usually incorporates a degree of role play and case-study methods.

- **On-the-job training:** On-the-job training (OJT) is probably the most often used instructional method. Some organizations realize they are using it, but others—those that have an employees' probation period—may not realize that they're using it. OJT is intended to be mentoring in its purest form. Instructional designers must ensure that this method does not preclude use of others.

- **Brainstorming:** This method asks learners to build experience into creativity by developing ideas on a specific subject with other colleagues. It can be tough to pull off and sometimes even tougher to design because it is freewheeling. Brainstorming sessions should never last more than 10 minutes, and facilitators should be given enough ideas for refocusing if the group becomes lethargic. Designers need to accept the fact that brainstorming may backfire on the facilitator and that these sessions have the potential to have a negative impact on the success of the project if the process bogs down in political or emotional responses. For example, a group that is working to find new ideas for a marketing campaign may end up blaming engineering for never having the right product available when the market peaks. It becomes important, therefore, that a facilitator be prepared to nudge the group back on track and away from a negative ending.

Other methods that are related directly to technology are computer-based training, multimedia, interactive TV, teleconferencing, groupware, virtual reality, and employee performance support systems (EPSSs). Chapter 11 describes Web-based instruction.

Instructional Methods to Avoid

There are three instructional methods to avoid:

- **Undirected groups:** This method is usually little more than groups discussing a topic or subject matter with little or no direction by a facilitator. It is typically used to kill time and offers little, if any, instructional value.

- **Unguided missile:** This seldom-used method usually begins with this statement from the facilitator at a training session: "Now, let's decide what we are going to do today." Although it may appear that there is a positive in getting group consensus for objectives, the method is an abandonment of instructional principles.

- **Theory tantrums:** Instructors must not dwell on theory. Training courses can only stand the smallest bits of theory when they substantiate a point or set the groundwork for something that follows. Always turn theory into practice.

Types of Distribution Methods

A number of distribution methods are widely used for training. The ones presented here are just a starting point for the discussion:

- **Captive audience:** Otherwise known as *classroom training*, this is the most common way to administer training. It consists of one or more learners with one or more facilitators in a single location using no technologies.
- **Technology enhanced:** This is the name for training that makes use of an overhead, slide projector, or laptop and computer projector. One or more technologies assist in the implementation of the course.
- **Technology facilitated:** This is what is commonly referred to by several hundred different terms such as **multimedia, CBT, e-learning,** and **virtual reality.** This platform is delivered with the technology, learner, and perhaps a facilitator in one location with the technology serving the dominant role in facilitation.
- **Distance learning:** This term describes the method in which learners are at one or more different physical locations than the source of the instruction. Teleconferencing is an example of distance learning.
- **Distributed learning:** Home study courses are an example of this method. Training is distributed by a process, such as by mail, that is not related to the implementation.

Other distribution methods include cable TV, CD-ROM, e-mail, extranets, Internet, intranets, LANs, satellite TV, simulators, voicemail, wide area networks, and the World Wide Web.

Learning technologies may be **synchronous** or **asynchronous.**

- **Synchronous** assumes that the learning and the facilitation take place at the same time. A good example is a chat room on the Internet. Everyone is participating in real time, and learners are usually expected to participate at a set time, much as a regular training course.

- **Asynchronous** training allows late sleepers and night owls to participate in training. Learners have a choice of when they participate as
one benefit of the technology. Learning is sometimes implemented as
an email system or a forum on a computer server.

When Should Training Be Revised?

Since the inception of the atomic age, most of us have become familiar with
the term **half-life.** It refers to how long half of the atoms in a radioactive substance will continue to emit radiation before they disintegrate. It has also
taken on a more cultural meaning. For instructional designers, the term refers
to the fact that data gathered in analysis has a half-life, or period of validity.
In some topic areas, the useful life of the data is measured in centuries. In others, it can literally be measured in seconds or minutes. In instructional design,
half-life means the time it takes for a noticeable or significant change in data
to take place.

It is important to note that this does not apply to all of the data becoming
useless, but only enough of it to render the training suspect or dated. It may
only take one incorrect element of the subject matter to ruin weeks of work
by a designer. This obsolescence is particularly noticeable in computer and
Web-based instruction. It is not uncommon for the design project to outlast
the technology. A designer may, for example, design a computer-based training project on the basis of a certain hardware and software platform that
could easily be at least a generation old when it is implemented.

To prevent this technology advancement from affecting a design, designers should ask the following data-decay rating questions for each element of
the project that may be affected. Respond with a rating from 0 to 5 (lowest to
highest):

- How critical are the data to the success of the training?
- How likely is it that the data will change?
- How easy is it to update data internally?
- Can learners or trainers easily obtain updated data?

If the analysis of the decay rating elements ends up being in the low end
of the scale, designers should consider a process that allows for updating.
This can be as easy as providing a Webpage for updated information or dis-
tributing data sheets as necessary. In either case, designers should not
assume that a completed project will rest comfortably on the information provided, unless they have determined that to be case.

Common Problems and Solutions

Too Much or Too Little Content

Instructional designers rarely have the luxury of exactly matching the amount of content with the time available for implementation. It is common for designers to have three days of content for a two-hour implementation requirement or 20 minutes of content for an eight-hour window. An effective way to solve the information overload problem is for the designer to call a meeting of all stakeholders in the training and marshal all the facts and data possible about the training.

At the meeting, the designer should take the following steps toward a consensus decision on the content:

- Cluster the data into topic areas.
- Prioritize the topic areas.
- Prioritize the data within each topic area.
- Decide which topics and subtopics cannot be eliminated.
- Review all topics and subtopics for redundancy.
- Combine and eliminate subtopics as necessary.
- Estimate timing on the topic areas and on each subtopic.
- Map out a project plan and outline each topic with the subtopics underneath them.
- Delineate the topics and subtopics with time indications so that it is obvious which ones will remain using different options.

If too little content remains, designers should review what they have to make sure they aren't missing something. If nothing is missing, they should try breaking the topics down into smaller chunks to see if it is possible to include more. It may also be possible to shorten the implementation time. It is never a good idea to waste a learner's time. Everyone knows when instructors are stretching content. Designers need to offer realistic expectations for keeping this problem from surfacing.

When Training Is Mandated

Mandated training is an exception to the rules for both too much and too little information. Designers often have little leeway in designing around obvious mismatches. Designers should think about these things before they move to the design stage:

- Have you really determined the problem, gap, or need?
- Have you determined if it is training or nontraining?
- Have you gathered data?
- Have you considered using one or all of these analysis methods to gather data?
  — focus group
  — surveys
  — task analysis
  — subject matter expert group

- Who are your subject matter experts?
- What are the constraints and resources?
- Have you determined all of the organizational needs?
- Have you reviewed your distribution and instructional methods?
- Do you know the half-life of your content?
- Do you have too much or too little content?

In Conclusion

In this chapter, you have learned about the analysis stage of instructional systems design. During analysis, designers must determine the answers to seven crucial questions. They must determine the need for instructional design and decide whether training is the right intervention for responding to that need. Their analyses requires them to explore the goals of the training and to gather information from population analyses, focus groups, surveys, and other sources. During this stage, they will conduct task analyses, which will help them to formulate the structure of their projects, and they will consider which instructional methods make sense. Before they begin designing their project, designers must also consider whether it is likely to be dated. Analysis requires a broad look ahead.

Putting What You Have Learned Into Action

Now, let's work through some analysis exercises to build your confidence and start you on the road to designing a project of your own. The exercises that follow cover these topics:

✓ Determining the need

✓ Population analysis

✓ Surveys

✓ Conducting a task analysis

✓ Choosing the right instructional method

✓ Knowing when to revise a project

✓ Getting ready for design.

If you have any trouble, go back to the appropriate section in the book for review.

Exercise 2.1. Poison prevention course, part 2. Determining the need.

When performing analysis, instructional designers must ask what the need is and whether training is the right solution. Is your need identified with nontraining problems such as wages, work conditions (environment), work procedures, or individual personnel issues? Or is it a need that includes acquiring or improving knowledge or skills?

1. The poison prevention course will be implemented in a community setting.

    a. Do you agree that the need clearly calls for training? _____

    _____

    b. Are there ways that you believe poison prevention training could be accomplished that do not involve training? What are they? _____

    _____

    Analysis found that a curriculum that provides both knowledge and skills is most likely to lead to a decrease in poisoning accidents or injuries from any accidents. For example:

    • Knowledge would include: poisoning, prevention methods, antidotes, 800 hot line number.

    • Skills would include: moving poisons out of the reach of children and pets, locking cabinets and drawers, giving antidotes.

This is clearly an instructional issue and can best be addressed with a training solution.

(continued on next page)

Exercise 2.1. Poison prevention course, part 2. Determining the need. *(continued)*

2. Now let's look at another type of project. An organization is moving to a new computer system that includes software and hardware. What questions would you ask to determine if training may be required? Two questions have been provided to get you started.

   a. Are the computers using a new operating system or newer version of the old operating system?

   b. What new software will be purchased?

   c. _____

   d. _____

3. What new knowledge and skills do you expect employees will need to acquire before they are able to use the new software successfully? Two answers have been provided to get you started.

Knowledge

   a. Background information concerning operating systems and new types of equipment in the system such as a scanner or printer and their function in a computer system

   b. _____

   c. _____

Skills

   a. ability to use a mouse, scanner, or new type of printer

   b. _____

   c. _____

Exercise 2.2. Poison prevention course, part 3. Population analysis.

In this exercise, you will analyze a population for a course. This example shows what a population analysis for the poison prevention course might look like. After you've reviewed it, go to the next exercise where you can choose a population that you are presently working with or one that you make up. The important element of this exercise is that you have an opportunity to observe at least a segment of your audience.

Poison prevention course:

1. Course name: <u>Poison Prevention in the Home</u>
2. Subject matter:<u> Poison prevention</u>
3. Intended audience:<u> General community</u>
4. Age range: <u>NA</u>
   Does it matter?<u> No</u>
5. Education range: <u>Mostly high school graduates and higher</u>
   Does it matter? <u>Yes, they need to be able to read the materials handed out in the course.</u>
6. Why would this population be interested in taking this course? <u>To protect their family and pets.</u>
7. Why would this population not be interested in taking this course? <u>Takes too much time or requires too much effort</u>
8. What is there about this population that has the potential to make this course a success? <u>Participants are interested in protecting their families.</u>
9. What is there about this population that has the potential to ruin this course? <u>Nothing</u>
10. Other distinguishing characteristics of this population: <u>Attendees will self-select to attend.</u>
11. Other Concerns
    - Ethnicity:<u> no</u>
    - Gender:<u> no</u>
    - Language:<u> no</u>
    - Literacy:<u> probably no</u>
    - Cost:<u> no, it is free</u>
    - Implementation time (when it is offered): <u>maybe, it will be offered at night</u>
    - Implementation length (course length):<u> no</u>
    - Internal or external politics:<u> no</u>
    - Transportation:<u> probably not, courses will be offered in community centers on bus routes</u>
    - ADA (Americans with Disability Act): <u>all sites are ADA compatible</u>
    - Motivation:<u> no, should be motivated</u>
    - Culture:<u> no</u>
    - What do I still not know about this population that I should know? <u>nothing that might prove to be a problem</u>

Exercise 2.3. Population analysis.

Now it's your turn. Using the population analysis for the poison prevention course as a guide, construct a population analysis for your course.

1. Course name: _____
2. Subject matter:_____
3. Intended audience:_____
4. Age range:_____
   Does it matter?_____
5. Education range: _____
   Does it matter? _____
   _____

6. Why would this population be interested in taking this course? _____
   _____

7. Why would this population not be interested in taking this course? _____
   _____

8. What is there about this population that has the potential to make this course a success?_____

9. What is there about this population that has the potential to ruin this course?_____

10. Other distinguishing characteristics of this population:_____
    _____

11. Other Concerns
    - Ethnicity:_____
    - Gender:_____
    - Language:_____
    - Literacy:_____
    - Cost: _____
    - Implementation time (when it is offered): _____
      _____
    - Implementation length (course length):_____
    - Internal or external politics:_____
    - Transportation:_____
      _____
    - ADA (Americans with Disability Act):_____
    - Motivation:_____
    - Culture:_____
    - What do I still not know about this population that I should know?
      _____

Exercise 2.4. Poison prevention course, part 4. Surveys.

Surveys are a great way to gather information. For the poison prevention course, we want to ask our population several questions about the course. The survey includes the following questions:

1. Do you feel as though your house could be safer for your family and pets when it comes to storing poisons?

   ☐ Yes   ☐ Maybe   ☐ No

2. Would you be interested in attending a one-hour course on poison prevention?

   ☐ Yes   ☐ Maybe   ☐ No

3. Do you know the Poison Prevention Hot Line's phone number?

   ☐ Yes   ☐ No

Exercise 2.5. Surveys.

Here's your chance to start asking questions for a project you need to complete. Use the space provided to design a survey of no more than five questions.

1. _____
   _____

2. _____
   _____

3. _____
   _____

4. _____
   _____

5. _____
   _____

Exercise 2.6. Surveys.

Here's another chance to practice. Design a survey of no more than five questions for gauging opinions about your course.

1. _____

   _____

2. _____

   _____

3. _____

   _____

4. _____

   _____

5. _____

   _____

Exercise 2.7. Poison prevention course, part 5. Conducting a task analysis.

In this exercise, you will perform a task analysis about police work. Police officers perform a multitude of assignments that require the four categories we have established—job, task, skill, and subskill. The job for task analysis purposes will be jailer. A jailer faces many challenges, the least of which is booking new prisoners after an arrest. The task for analysis will be fingerprinting an arriving prisoner.

Fingerprinting requires many skills, which may vary from one police station to another depending on the equipment and departmental procedures. The skill of correctly placing the fingers on the recording medium (usually either a piece of heavy paper or a scanner attached to a computer system) requires a number of subskills.

Subskills need to be identified and recorded in a manner that will allow designers to develop that information into objectives and evaluation tasks. As we observe the process of fingerprinting, we need to keep this in mind.

Someone who observes fingerprinting in order to perform a task analysis would see the following steps in the process:

- The prisoner's fingers are cleaned with a disposable cloth that contains a cleaning solution.
- The prisoner's first finger (or thumb) is placed in an ink solution.
- The jailer checks to see that the entire finger is covered with ink.
- The prisoner's finger is placed firmly on the paper and then rolled across the paper so that the entire print appears on the paper.
- The jailer continues with the remaining fingers and thumbs until all 10 digits are recorded.
- The prints are reviewed to ensure that all are recorded correctly.
- The prisoner's fingers are again cleaned.
- The prisoner is returned to a cell.

As that person observes the process, he or she would also develop a list of questions, such as the following:

- What is the cleaning solution that is used before the ink is placed on the prisoner's fingers?
- How much ink is applied to each finger or thumb?
- Is there any particular order to taking the prints?
- How do you determine that a print is good?

Once the task analysis is completed, it is time to reduce the observations into behaviors that will be used to write objectives. Let's look at the list below derived from our observations.

- **Job:** Jailer
- **Task:** Fingerprinting a new prisoner
- **Skill:** Making a fingerprint
- **Subskills:**
  — Clean fingers.
  — Placing fingers in ink.
  — Check for ink coverage on fingers.
  — Place fingers on paper.
  — Review each print.
  — Clean prisoner's fingers.

(continued on next page)

Exercise 2.7. Poison prevention course, part 5. Conducting a task analysis. *(continued)*

Now we have prepared a list of behaviors that will serve as one element of our objectives to be written later in the design process. For example, a behavior statement from the observed data indicating that a jailer needs to place the prisoner's finger on the paper would read "should be able to place the prisoner's finger on the paper." Now, we are building the objective from the observations in the task analysis process. The next chapter provides more information about objectives, but this is one source of the information you will need to write objectives for a course.

Exercise 2.8. Conducting a task analysis.

Now think about a project you are working on and pick a job, task, and skill and write them in the spaces that follow. After you have done this, divide the skill into subskills, as shown in the fingerprinting example, and list them in the allotted spaces:

- **Job:**_____

- **Task:** _____

- **Skill:**_____

- **Subskills:** _____

Exercise 2.9. Choosing the right instructional method.

If you have determined that you have an instructional need, it is important to look at possible instructional methods you might consider to meet that need. Several to consider include lecture, role play, case study, simulations, gaming, critical incident, drill, job aid, critique, discussion, on-the-job training, and brainstorming.

For the poison prevention course, the best combination of instructional methods to meet our goal of preventing poisonings appears to be lectures, discussions, brainstorming, and job aids. These four methods satisfy the specific needs on the basis of the population, implementation setting, and course length. Lecture works best because subject matter needs to be presented to the participants in a timely fashion. Discussion allows participants to be part of the fun and brings ownership to the process for them. Brainstorming brings solutions to each participant's particular needs within the course.

If you are using this book to help build your own course or even as a sanity check for a course you have already designed, consider each of these methods listed in table 3 and determine which ones would best meet your instructional needs. Put a check mark in the box for yes if the method would and in the box for no if the method would not, and state the reason. Space is available to add any other methods that make sense for your needs.

Table 3. Choosing an instructional method.

Method	Yes	No	Reason
Lecture			
Role play			
Case study			
Simulations			
Gaming			
Critical incident			
Drill			
Job aid			
Critique			
Discussion			
In-basket			
On-the-job training			
Brainstorming			
Others			

Exercise 2.10. Knowing when to revise a project.

One important aspect of analysis is determining when a project should be revised. This is true when first designing a project and also if you are reviewing the need for a project to be updated. Here are the critical questions to ask yourself:

- How critical are the data to the success of the training?
- How likely is it that the data will change?
- How easy is it for trainers to update the data internally?
- Can learners or trainers easily obtain updated data?

For the poison prevention course, we can answer the questions like this based on a 0 to 5 scale (lowest to highest) :

- How critical are the data to the success of the training? The answer is a five because the data are critical to give participants the life-saving information they need.
- How likely is it that the data will change? This is probably a five given the rapidly changing list of poisons that might harm someone.
- How easy is it for trainers to update the data internally? This is a four because it should be easy to access updated information as it becomes available.
- Can learners or trainers easily obtain updated data? This is a one or two because the trainers or learners must make the effort to get the updates, and they may not be willing or able to access them. They may have to get on the Internet or call a long-distance number. You can't expect much updating by the end users after the project is distributed and implemented unless the sponsoring organization supplies the updates.

From this set of answers, it is clear that updating this project is vitally important. The data are critical to the training. Data including phone numbers and poison listings are likely to change. It must be easy for trainers to update the data internally, so subject matter experts will probably have to be involved in the future updates to ensure quality.

So, for this project we can make yearly updates an integral part of our design strategy.

Now, consider a project you are working on. How will you rate these four questions?

- How critical is the data to the success of the training? _____
- How likely is it that the data will change? _____
- How easy is it for trainers to update the data internally? _____
- Can learners or trainers easily obtain updated data? _____

Exercise 2.11. Getting ready for design.

Analysis is the foundation for the rest of your project. You need to assemble some important information before you move on to the design element of ISD. Take a look at the bulleted points below and state whether you have completed each step. Explain where necessary. Your project cannot be successful without this information.

- Subject matter for your project
  ☐ Yes   ☐ No

- Determine the need or problem
  ☐ Yes   ☐ No

- Determine if it is training or nontraining
  ☐ Yes   ☐ No

- Determine organizational goals
  ☐ Yes   ☐ No

- Determine resources
  ☐ Yes   ☐ No

- Determine obstacles
  ☐ Yes   ☐ No

- Prepare a population profile
  ☐ Yes   ☐ No

- Conduct a focus group if necessary
  ☐ Yes   ☐ No

- Conduct a task analysis if necessary
  ☐ Yes   ☐ No

- Make sure you have all the information you need to write objectives and evaluation tasks in the design phase.
  ☐ Yes   ☐ No

3

Design: Writing Objectives

Chapter Objectives

At the conclusion of this chapter, you should be able to:

- write four-part objectives
- differentiate between terminal and enabling objectives
- describe the four different objective domains
- define the performance agreement principle
- explain what interactivity is.

Writing Objectives

The single most important skill a designer can learn is how to write objectives. Whether known as behavioral or performance objectives or exit competencies or expected outcomes, objectives are the keystone of instructional design. Anyone who can write objectives has the potential to accomplish anything in the field of training or education.

ISD centers on the concept of objectives. Objectives are the nucleus of every other aspect of instructional design. Designers who can write excellent four-part objectives will not have trouble with the other elements of the process. By the same token, if a designer's project seems unbalanced or some aspects of it are not working, he or she should look at the objectives. Too many design problems start with sloppy objectives. Valuing the components embodied in objectives forces a designer to transform vague goals into observable behaviors.

Basics of Objectives

Designers frame objectives from the perspective of the end user of the training, not the facilitator. They do not say what a facilitator is supposed to do, but what the learner should be able to do at the end of the course. It would not be correct to say, "The facilitator will teach the students how to use the fax machine" or "At the end of this course, the facilitator will have presented all of the course materials in a friendly and persuasive manner." Learners are the focus of objectives because they are the reason for the course. Although directions to a facilitator are important to instructional design, they say nothing about what the leaner is supposed to do at the end of the course.

Objectives are written at the level of an individual learner. Writing an objective that describes more than one learner presents a number of design issues, the least of which is how designers provide any meaningful evaluation. It is also problematic for a designer to think of an entire subset of learners as if they were a single learner. To do so challenges clarity. An objective for a group project can easily be written at the level of the single learner. Following is an objective for a group:

> Given paint, brushes, and a bare wall, the apprentices in the Painting for Pleasure course will create a mural with the dimensions of at least 4 feet by 4 feet.

It should be stated as follows:

> Given paint, brushes, and a bare wall, an apprentice in the Painting for Pleasure course will create a mural element with other apprentices who contribute at least one section of the completed work.

The second objective makes it possible for each learner to be evaluated on his or her individual accomplishment, without relying on other learners. Following is a learner-centered version of an objective on use of a fax machine:

> Given a working fax machine, the Office Technology participant should be able to send a two page fax to another location without error.

Objectives are necessary for each learning activity. Every concept, skill, or objective-worthy behavior needs to be identified and honored with an objective. If an activity is important enough to be included in a design plan, then it is important enough to have a written objective. An objective is the best way to guarantee that the designer will evaluate whether course participants have mastered each skill or concept for which there is instruction. Designers have a tendency to write either too many or too few objectives. They can decide if they need to write an objective by answering the question, "Does it stand on its own?"

Objectives Are Not Goals

Goals and objectives are not the same things. Goals are general statements of desired outcomes, whereas **objectives** are detailed statements of outcomes. For example, a goal might be to improve communications within an organization, whereas an objective for that goal might be

> Given several role-play situations and class discussions, the Better Communications participant should be able to develop at least three specific ways to improve intraoffice communications.

Designers should write objectives so that they can be met within the implementation time of the course. This is a nice way of saying, "Don't promise something you have no control over." Setting an objective that states that a learner "... should be able to construct an effective marketing plan" is much different than an objective that promises "increased sales in six months." Designers only have control over the process of training a learner to assemble a marketing plan, not the sales volume.

What Objectives Should Be

Objectives should be measurable and observable. An objective that cannot be measured or observed is probably not going to have much chance for evaluation. That shortcoming significantly diminishes the usefulness of the objective.

There are a number of different methods for writing objectives. The most recognized format contains the elements of audience, behavior, condition, and degree. It is known as the **A-B-C-D format,** for the first letter of each of the words. Some other formats require a fifth element, whereas still others require only three. The adding and subtracting of elements is usually the result of adding more detail to a behavior or eliminating the audience element.

The Four Elements of an Objective

Theorists and practitioners have used a variety of formats for objectives. ISD allows designers to adjust their process to meet their needs, and not all of them use the A-B-C-D format. However, designers should never undertake the process of designing objectives without reviewing the four elements as part of the procedure. If they consider audience, behavior, condition, and degree as they design their objectives, they are halfway to a successful design. Following are descriptions of each of the elements.

Audience

What must appear as the most obvious of the objective elements—the audience—is crucial to writing them. Designers must validate the audience for each objective. Just as the term **student** may refer to someone in kindergarten or high school, so may the terms **learner** and **participant.** Designers must make sure that the audience statement is specific to the course and intended population.

The description should be specific by using the course title or another characteristic, such as:

- The New Methods in Marketing participant
- learner in Handling Stress on the Job
- Local 786 apprentice painter
- Software for Cynics student.

The designer must validate the audience for each objective.

Behavior

Without any meaningful statement of behavior, both objectives and training itself become pointless. Behavior is the culmination of all the analysis and the purpose for evaluation.

A close examination of a behavior statement in an objective reveals a vivid description of an anticipated outcome. When trainers predict that a learner should be able to do anything, the designer is establishing the finish line for every learner.

Most behavior statements are worded in the format "should be able to _____" or "will be able to _____." Designers must be careful about which of these formats they choose for writing their objectives. **Will** and **should** have two distinctly different meanings, and the selection is more than just stylistic. Promising that a learner will be able to do something is much different than stating one should be able to something. The argument against **will** is based on the concept of promising absolute results. For example, if an objective states that the "Golfing for Beginners participant will be able to score in the low 60s for 18 holes of golf," the designer better have one great golf program developed. **Designers better not make promises they cannot keep.**

The behavior statement must not use verbs such as **learn** and **understand** because there is no way to measure or observe them. Just because a learner's frequent nods and thoughtful looks give the facilitator reason to believe that he or she is learning and understanding, that does not make it true. Behavior needs to be observable and measurable. Verbs like **create,**

write, list, construct, and **repair** are observable, measurable, and suitable for statements of behavior in written objectives.

Observable and Measurable Verbs

Following are examples of verbs that work well in behavior statements:

Apply	Employ	Rank
Argue	Estimate	Rearrange
Assess	Examine	Recognize
Calculate	Explain	Record
Change	Express	Relate
Choose	Extrapolate	Repeat
Cite	Formulate	Rephrase
Classify	Identify	Report
Combine	Illustrate	Restate
Compare	Infer	Schedule
Conclude	Integrate	Score
Contrast	Interpolate	Sketch
Criticize	Interpret	Solve
Decide	Inventory	Specify
Define	Judge	Standardize
Derive	Manage	Tell
Design	Measure	Translate
Diagram	Name	Transmit
Differentiate	Operate	Underline
Discuss	Organize	Use
Dramatize	Prescribe	Validate
Draw up a list	Question	

Statements involving psychomotor behavior include **pull, hold, turn, tighten,** and **rotate.** Don't worry about not seeing these verbs and others like them in the list of behaviors. They are obvious enough not to require listing.

Condition

The objectives in the earlier examples begin with the word **given.** Objectives need to state the givens to ensure that learners have a complete and consistent foundation from which to work. The condition statement in an objective clearly delineates the conditions for a given behavior. Conditions may include tangible things, like tools, books, equipment, or hardware; they may also have their basis in an instructional method.

For example, a condition might say "given a screwdriver and 10 screws" or "provided with a 1329A test set." Other less tangible conditions are "... following participation in a role play" or "... after having read chapter 4 of the text."

Although it may appear that condition statements are either too obvious to be useful or overly complicated, subtle differences in context can sink an otherwise great course. Some facilitators may omit books or other reading material, and instructional methods intended for the course might be replaced or eliminated based on a facilitator's whim. The omission of mention of a specific book, other reading material, or an instructional method may seem insignificant, but it may result in a facilitator's taking a different approach to teaching. General condition statements, such as "when completed with this course," are inadequate because they do not provide any foundation from which to work. Try to be as thorough as possible in setting the context.

In the poison prevention course, for example, the conditions might be the following:

- given a planning sheet and sketch of a home or office
- after working with another participant in the course
- provided several real-life scenarios of potential poisoning hazards.

Each of these provides the context that supports the other elements of an objective.

Degree

The degree statement is the instructional design equivalent to a price tag in retail: It sets the price. A learner will feel frustrated if he or she does not know what it takes to meet an objective.

Writing degree statements is like playing the game of horseshoes. The object of the game is to place the horseshoe's open end around a pole and get a set number of points. Players can also accumulate fewer points for being within a certain distance of the pole, usually the length of the horseshoe.

The object of learning is to meet an objective. A learner should be able to score some points even if he or she does not hit the mark. As instructional designers write their objectives, they need to be clear about how close a learner needs to get to meet them. The difficulty in writing degree statements is in the process of realistically setting the degree threshold. Some examples of degree statements are as follows:

- successfully three times
- without error
- within five minutes
- on three different models of the equipment
- by offering an opinion
- a learning contract
- a grade of 70 percent or better on the quiz
- five-minute speech on a topic of her choosing
- at least five baskets from the three-point line
- a rating of nine or above as scored by a panel of judges.

All of these degree statements meet the criterion of being a good objective element because they are observable and measurable. No doubt should exist in anyone's mind about what needs to be done to meet the objective.

A number of degree statements come close, but are not really adequate. These statements include:

- at the discretion of the instructor
- after participating
- at the end of the course.

Instructional designers should also be careful with statements that include ambiguous words like **safely, carefully, honestly,** and other adverbs. It is tough to avoid some of these words, but they require additional clarifying information if they are put in an objective. The word **safely,** for example, would not be measurable in the phrase "use the machine safely," but would be measurable used this way:

> . . . will be performed safely, as documented in the Occupational Safety and Health Administration (OSHA) 500 standards.

It is also necessary to use percentages carefully in degree statements. A passing grade of 85 percent or better on the final exam is fine as a degree. However, a cardiopulmonary resuscitation (CPR) class that says students will be able to perform CPR correctly 85 percent of the time would not be an acceptable threshold. In certain skill sets anything less than 100 percent proficiency is questionable. Percentages must be reasonable. It is better to have an employee of a coffee shop meet an objective of making four acceptable lattes in a row, rather than one of operating the latte machine correctly at least 70 percent of the time.

Terminal and Enabling Objectives

Terminal objectives are the final behavioral outcomes of a specific instructional event. For a course on the safe handling of asbestos on a job site, a terminal objective might be as follows:

> Given a realistic scenario depicting the handling and disposal of asbestos at a work site, the participant in the asbestos supervisors course should be able to supervise the work of at least two asbestos removal technicians. The participant must comply with all OSHA standards that relate to the specific situation depicted in the scenario. No deficiency will be allowed, and the participant must repeat the process until able to comply with the zero-deficiency standard.

This description clearly states the skill the participant should have at the end of the course. There can be as many terminal objectives as needed, whether one or a thousand. In large projects, instructional designers can end up with design plans that fit in a series of three-ring binders, but it is also possible to have just one. The number varies with the design needs.

Enabling objectives support the terminal objectives. In the asbestos example, the supervisor would have to perform all the tasks that will be taught. Following are two possible enabling objectives that show use of the equipment and tools of the asbestos technician:

> Given a hammer and chisel, and while suited, the technician should be able to remove sprayed asbestos from a wall or ceiling without being exposed to the asbestos dust.

> Given a bag of asbestos materials collected on the work site, the technician should be able to dispose of the material in the removal containers without any leakage of material.

Format of Terminal and Enabling Objectives

There are a number of different ways to write and format the two types of objectives. Terminal objectives have audience, behavior, condition, and degree components, but enabling objectives do not need the audience element. Some instructional designers insist that enabling objectives should read more like an evaluation task, as in the following example:

> While wearing the proper clothing, the technician will use a hammer and chisel to safely remove asbestos.

How instructional designers may write and format their objectives is up to them. Sometimes it is a good practice to combine elements of a terminal objective with those of an enabling objective to provide a much more readable format, as in the following example:

Given all required tools and safety equipment, the participant in the asbestos supervisor course should be able to:

- remove asbestos, without exposure, wearing proper safety equipment
- remove debris from the work site using the proper containers without any leakage of material.

It is important to be certain to have all the objectives in the proper order. In the previous example, the participant must wear the proper equipment before removing debris, so that objective comes first.

Objective Domains

Objective domains are categories of objectives that assist instructional designers in determining a number of important design elements. The four objective domains are cognitive, affective, psychomotor, and interpersonal. Primarily, they assist instructional designers in determining how to structure objectives, evaluations, and delivery systems.

Designers seldom mix objectives and evaluation tasks from different objective domains because they may then lack validity. The following description shows their importance to designers without going into the science of objective domains.

An instructional designer who was working on a training program for technicians to repair a certain type of computer might use all four domains in the following way in the design process:

- **Cognitive domain:** A learner should be able to know how to repair the equipment set.
- **Psychomotor domain:** A learner should be able to physically remove cases and insert boards and should be able to perform other skills requiring the use of the body.
- **Affective domain:** Learners should be able to offer strategies to overcome negative feelings about repairing certain models.
- **Interpersonal domain:** Learners should be able to provide excellent customer service.

Following is a description of each domain in detail.

Cognitive Domain

The cognitive domain will probably account for most of an instructional designer's objectives. Generally, the definition of **cognitive domain** in training is the cognitive, or thought, actions of the brain that result from the act of processing sensory. The cognitive domain can be thought of as the output from a process. One could argue successfully that every objective will probably have some component of the cognitive domain. The distinction between domains becomes important because of overlaps like this. The output of the behavior is the point at which instructional designers can judge the predominant domain. For example, if the output from a behavior is mostly the processing of data, then the domain would be cognitive. Following are examples of objectives in the cognitive domain:

The learner should be:

- able to distinguish the difference between circuit board 14R and 17Y
- able to add and subtract fractions
- able to identify risk factors associated with hepatitis
- able to recite the organizational oath.

The learner must take cognitive actions to meet each one of these objectives.

Psychomotor Domain

The psychomotor domain is undoubtedly the easiest one to identify. If an objective mainly requires movement, it is probably psychomotor. Learning to operate a machine or using a computer mouse are two examples of skills that are in the psychomotor domain. Although they both have some cognitive influence, they require movement for successful completion of the objective.

Here are some objectives for psychomotor behaviors:

The learner should be

- able to change the toner cartridge in the copy machine
- able to assemble circuit pack 2349
- able to repair a broken antenna on a field radio
- able to attach option 7T to the main assembly.

Interpersonal Domain

Many of the soft skill training programs in large organizations are in some way related to the interaction of two or more individuals. This is why interpersonal behaviors are important. Designers are often forced into playing mediator in organizational disputes between individuals or departments. This is often related to interpersonal problems and requires a separate objective set.

Examples of objectives involving interpersonal behaviors include:

The learner should be:

- able to identify an area of disagreement between the two departments
- able to answer the phone and take a message without displaying obvious anger or impatience

- able to participate in a role-play situation reflecting the key areas of conflict in the office
- able to answer a question without resorting to name calling.

Affective Domain

Objectives in this domain are soft skills that are difficult to observe and measure. Constructing evaluation tasks for affective domains is difficult and may be the reason that some designers shy away from writing this objective.

Many instructional designers think it is nearly impossible to write a behavior statement for some affective domain objectives. Others argue that you cannot change the way someone "feels" about a subject. It is not easy, but it is usually possible to work effectively as a designer in these behaviors. The designer cannot work to change a learner's attitude, just the learner's behavior. For example, a training program on customer service for new clerks in a retail environment would have affective domain objectives. If the goal of the training is to influence behavior and not the interpersonal aspects of the issue (that is, how a clerk tells a customer that 32-inch jeans do not comfortably fit a 48-inch waist), an instructional designer would write objectives for affective domain behaviors. An affective domain objective for this situation might be stated like this:

> The learner in the New Clerks Training will describe at least two anger-displacement strategies in a case study situation involving a customer being aggressive about a return with no receipt.

The intent of this behavior statement is to get the new clerk to process the anger and maintain composure in this difficult situation, which the clerk will likely face on the job. It certainly is not the intent of the objective to keep the clerk from wanting to confront the customer.

Affective domain objectives and the issues associated with trying to operationalize the process will always be difficult. It can be very hard to separate behavior from the trigger that brings the response, and that is a challenge designers constantly face. Workplace violence is a good example of an affective domain issue.

A strategy for the training is to address individual worker's violent tendencies, and that involves affective domain. Helping supervisors deal with potentially violent workers before violence erupts addresses the interpersonal domain. Clearly there are elements of all four domains at work in these examples. However, the focus is on one domain, whereas the others play an enabling role.

Following is how an objective might be written for the affective domain in the workplace violence example:

> Given a stop-action role-play situation in which the Workplace Violence participant assumes the role of a worker who feels anger at another worker on the job, the participant should be able to successfully articulate at least two strategies to keep his or her anger under control when the role play stops for discussion.

Following is how an objective might be written for the interpersonal domain in the workplace violence example:

> Given a role-play situation in which the Workplace Violence Prevention for Supervisors participant assumes the role of a supervisor who is facilitating a potentially violent workplace confrontation, the learner should be able to enact a strategy that prevents the situation from moving from confrontation to violence.

The difference in these two is the focus of the objective. One approach intends to work within the emotional framework of the individual, whereas the other relies on interpersonal skills to diffuse a violent situation. Both have the same long-term goal of stopping violence, but they approach it in very different ways.

Using Objective Domains in the Design Process

Instructional designers should think about the following once they establish their primary objective domain:

- **Consistency throughout their design in domain-related areas.** These areas include performance agreement, materials, instructional methods, evaluation techniques, and any design elements that are influenced by domain. Crossing domains will disrupt the design and confuse or negate the objectives.

  For example, objectives written for a training program that will instruct paramedics in the use of a defibrillator are probably going to be psychomotor. The designer's objectives and course design should stay largely in that domain. If the course actually ends up focusing on the emotional trauma associated with being a first responder, the designer has switched domains and endangered the original goal of the course, the use of a defibrillator.

- **Consistency with analysis data.** Designers should not cross domains when moving from analysis to design. They must not ignore analysis data through the misreading of predominant domain.

  For example, in a course for paramedics, if the analysis data show that learners are worried about learning when and if to use the siren and lights on the ambulance, the topic of the final course should not focus on how to use specific brands and models of sirens and lights. Rather, the topic should be when-and-if concerns about the use of sirens and lights.

Degree of Difficulty

A number of taxonomies suggest that certain behaviors are more difficult to learn than others. Predicting is more difficult than defining, for example, and distinguishing is less difficult than synthesizing.

A designer needs to know the **degrees of difficulty** in order to ensure that an objective follows a continuum from simple to complex or from easy to hard. Most learning theories suggest that moving a learner slowly up the slope of difficulty allows a gradual accumulation of information. People who are learning to play an instrument start with simple exercises to assist in learning the basics. As they acquire more skill, they move to playing sequences of notes and then to playing short melodies.

As designers develop their objectives and evaluation tasks, they must keep in mind the degree of difficulty of single objectives and then the sequencing of all the objectives in a project. A good practice is to assign a numerical value for difficulty from one to 10 and then to rate each objective. The objectives should begin with the lower numbers and proceed to the higher. By following that sequence, it would be easy for designers to see if they have a problem in their sequencing. In a course for running a marathon, for example, designers would sequence objectives in such a way that the less difficult skills or concepts are given in the beginning, and the more difficult are offered at the end. For example, an early objective might be for a participant to take short, one-kilometer runs every other day for a week. This is relatively easy compared with a terminal objective of running a 26-kilometer race and would probably rate a one or two, whereas a series of five-kilometer runs would be four or five. The terminal objective of running 26 kilometers would rate a maximum 10 in this series because it is the most difficult objective in the course.

Evaluation Tasks and the Performance Agreement Principle

The usefulness of objectives is severely jeopardized without evaluation tasks. In fact, it makes little sense to bother with objectives if there is no intention to evaluate a learner's progress toward meeting them. Designers must develop the ability to construct evaluation tasks. The tasks must not be a hurdle in themselves; they must be achievable and based on real life. Examples of simple evaluation tasks are as follows:

- Using the circuit pack labeled B-75, replace the defective processor board on the server and confirm that it is operating without error.
- You have until 4:00 p.m. to correctly solve all 25 math problems.

Evaluation tasks are created during the design phase to ensure that every objective has a corresponding learner-level evaluation as part of the course. Every objective needs to have this evaluation to ensure performance agreement.

Performance Agreement Principle

Performance agreement is a design term that describes the process of matching objectives and evaluation tasks together in a curriculum. This is a key concept in ISD because it mandates that objectives always have an evaluation and that evaluations always having an objective.

One of the reasons that ISD is so useful is that it sticks to a process. The correct use of ISD makes it almost impossible to leave out major chunks of curriculum design. Performance agreement insists that instructional designers pay careful attention to balance in their design work by insisting on an evaluation of every objective.

As an example, here is an objective written for a segment of a course called Sales for the Beginner:

> Given a realistic role-play situation with Sales for the Beginner, the learner playing the part of the salesperson should be able to present three reasons why the client should purchase a specific product.

With the objective written, the instructional designer will have to construct an evaluation task. Here is a suggested approach:

> You have just entered the office of a major client. You have to make a case for buying your top-line product. It is important that you present at least three reasons why the client should purchase your product.

The designer would then have to measure the performance agreement. The behavior, condition, and degree statements are the key elements the designer would have to match in the objective and the evaluation task. The first step in determining performance agreement is to identify these three elements in each. Table 4 shows each element in the objective and the evaluation task.

All of the behaviors, conditions, and degree statements agree. When they do, the designer has created a performance agreement.

Table 4. The performance agreement match.

	Objective	Evaluation Task
Behavior	. . . the learner . . . should be able to present . . . reasons why the client should purchase a specific product	. . . you present . . . reasons why the client should purchase your product
Condition	Given a realistic role-play situation with . . . learner playing the part of the salesperson . . .	You have just entered the office of a major client. You have to make a case for buying your top-line product.
Degree	. . . present three reasons . . .	. . . three reasons . . .

A good test of objectives is whether instructional designers are able to come up with an evaluation task. If it is not possible, the objective may be flawed in one or all of the three elements.

Correcting Performance Agreement Problems

The best way to fix problems with performance agreements is to change either the objective or the evaluation task to ensure the two are in agreement. Designers should base their decision about which to change on their analysis efforts and the context of their course. Consider the following objective:

> Provided with a stethoscope and blood pressure measuring equipment, the Nursing 304 student should be able to determine the blood pressure of five patients, as verified by the instructor.

If the evaluation task and objective did not agree, the designer could change the evaluation task to have the student take the blood pressure of all the patients. Another possibility would be to change the objective to include making a determination of need and then measuring the blood pressure of only those patients that need to have it done.

Take a look at the following example:

> Given participation in a role-play situation, the Effective Intercultural Communications student should be able to say hello and good-bye in at least two languages other than English.

If the evaluation task and objective did not agree, the designer could change the objective from the requirement for hello and good-bye fluency to something else, or the designer could rewrite the evaluation task to have the student saying hello in a large hotel lobby where numerous languages are being spoken.

Choosing Distribution and Instructional Methods

Making decisions about how a course will be implemented involves choosing the appropriate distribution and instructional methods. Designers must use data gathered in analysis to determine the best possible options. Every situation is different and requires a thorough appreciation of the pluses and minuses of each.

The most important rule for choosing distribution and instructional methods is simple and often overlooked: **Never choose a technology before you determine what works best for your design.**

A high-tech firm with worldwide facilities made the assumption that those who work at computers all day must want to have training delivered the same way. Luckily a thoughtful instructional designer had the foresight to survey the target population. The survey revealed that these learners wanted trainers to deliver the instruction in person instead of receiving technology-delivered training.

Plenty of examples can also be found when learners wanted technology-delivered training instead of the traditional lecture or one-on-one mentoring learning. The lessons here are obvious. It is important to find out how the learners want their training delivered.

Interactivity

Interactivity is the strength of instructional design, but it is also where it is most vulnerable. The definition of **interactivity** for this book is as follows:

> **Interactivity** is the trading of information between learner and mentor in a way that remains faithful to the design principles of performance agreement and objective domains.

The implication of this definition is that every training project must have an exchange of information between the learner and the provider of the information. The provider, or the mentor, can be a facilitator or a computer monitor or anything else. Interactivity is important for two simple reasons: Learners need to be challenged, and they need to have an opportunity to ask questions and receive answers.

Unfortunately, interactivity does not enter into enough instructional design projects. Too much training occurs by lecture, though it is a myth that learning is best achieved by osmosis. Learners do not make much progress toward meeting objectives while sleeping. It is up to instructional designers to see that sleeping is the result of exhaustion following a great training experience, not boredom.

Mentoring to Ensure Interactivity

Some people think of a mentor as someone who helps a younger person mature in his or her profession or personally—a wiser soul who takes the time to push, tug, or otherwise finesse a colleague toward a goal. When an instructional designer interjects the concept of mentoring into the design process, interactivity will happen. No matter how much technology a designer uses, the mentoring process should be part of the decision process. The same is true for the most basic captive audience courses. The mentoring concept offers another tool for the designer's tool kit. Here's how it works:

Imagine that you are working on a design project for middle managers who need help with delegation. It has taken years for them to decide to let you do it instead of doing it themselves. After careful analysis, you have determined that using an in-basket instructional method is the way to go. Your learners will be presented with a pile of simulated memos, letters, email, and phone messages to prioritize and delegate when necessary. They want it online so that they can access it whenever they get a chance.

You arrange for a simple Web-based training module, and as you are putting it together, you realize that you are going to have difficulty meeting objectives without interactivity. Realistically you cannot have someone standing around waiting for a manager to decide to have someone evaluate his or her work. You want to make it part of the Web-based component of the course, but the many variations that might arise limit your ability to do that within a small budget.

Your plan is to have the learners complete the Web-based component and for a report to be printed with each learner's decisions for the in-basket exercise. Each learner then arranges to meet with a facilitator to review the results. Your course design offers both asynchronous implementation and synchronous mentoring.

Here's another example:

A large financial firm is giving an expensive training course that is not meeting its goals. You are asked to review the course design and make recommendations for a fix.

The course, Customer Service Basics, is being implemented in a meeting room and presented in a lecture format. All employees who have contact with the public in each branch office must take the hour-long course. Your analysis shows that each employee has access to at least one computer terminal at each desk or counter.

Your recommendation is that you include objectives that may be missing in the one-hour training session and supplement with job aids that are posted on each computer monitor. Each job aid provides both text and audio examples of each element of the course and answers questions in customer-service-related problems from irate customers. Your mentoring is technology based but still provides interactivity and access.

In Conclusion

This chapter began the exploration of design. It covered the process of writing four-part objectives and explained how instructional designers use terminal and enabling objectives and the objective domains to make certain the objectives make sense. It explained how instructional designers adhere to the performance agreement principle to ensure they can assess the objectives. The chapter also explained the importance of interactive instruction.

The next chapter addresses the design of lesson plans, a crucial aspect of any instructional design project.

Putting What You Have Learned Into Action

Now, let's work through some exercises to build your confidence and start you on the road to designing a project of your own. The exercises that follow cover these topics:

- ✓ Writing objectives
- ✓ Determining audience, behavior, condition, and degree
- ✓ Writing terminal and enabling objectives
- ✓ Checking for performance agreement

Exercise 3.1. Poison prevention course, part 6. Writing objectives.

Now that you are familiar with the four parts of an objective, it is time to start writing them. Spend a little time reviewing the following examples from the poison prevention course. Remember that you can easily substitute the content to match your specific needs. After reviewing these examples, it is time for you to take a turn at writing objectives.

1. **Audience:** the Poison Prevention in the Home participant
   Behavior: should be able to create a plan to store poison
   Condition: given handouts, a job aid, and class discussion
   Degree: that removes any chance that children or pets can gain access to a poison.

   Combining them, the objective reads as follows:

   > Given handouts, a job aid, and class discussion, the Poison Prevention in the Home participant should be able to create a plan to store poisons that removes any chance that children or pets can gain access to a poison.

   Following is another example from that course.

2. **Audience:** Poison Prevention in the Home participant
   Behavior: should be able to make a map of his or her home
   Conditions: given a blank sheet of paper and a pencil
   Degree: depicting every location that now contains poisons

   So, it will look like this:

   > Given a blank sheet of paper and a pencil, the Poison Prevention in the Home participant should be able to make a map of his or her home depicting every location that now contains poisons.

Exercise 3.2. Writing objectives.

In the following exercises, write the objectives for the content and audience shown or substitute with content relevant to your own project. The first one is an example.

1. **Content:** quiet a squeaky door
   Audience: the Homeowner 101 participant
   Behavior: should be able to apply oil to the hinges of a squeaky door
   Condition: given a can of oil
   Degree: until it stops squeaking

(continued on next page)

Exercise 3.2. Writing objectives. *(continued)*

2. **Content:** answering a phone
   Audience: the Homeowner 101 participant should be able to
   Behavior: _____
   _____

   Condition: _____
   _____

   Degree: _____
   _____

3. **Content:** lighting a candle
   Audience: the Homeowner 101 participant should be able to
   Behavior: _____
   _____

   Condition: _____
   _____

   Degree: _____
   _____

4. **Content:** turning on an oven
   Audience: the Homeowner 101 participant should be able to
   Behavior: _____
   _____

   Condition: _____
   _____

   Degree: _____
   _____

5. **Content:** heating water in a microwave
   Audience: the Homeowner 101 participant should be able to
   Behavior: _____
   _____

   Condition: _____
   _____

   Degree: _____
   _____

Exercise 3.3. Writing terminal and enabling objectives.

You are designing a course for new toll takers on the turnpike. You have decided that the first module will be courtesy to drivers. Write at least two terminal and enabling objectives to support this 30-minute module. You may instead substitute this exercise with content relevant to your own project.

1. **Terminal objectives:**

   _____

   _____

   _____

   _____

   _____

   _____

2. **Enabling objectives:**

   _____

   _____

   _____

   _____

   _____

How did you do? Did your answer look like this:

1. **Terminal objectives:** The participant in the Toll Takers Introductory Course should be able to:
   - Demonstrate the three aspects of courtesy, defined in the toll takers handbook, when participating in a role-play situation and assuming the role of toll taker
   - Provide the proper change while deflecting the anger of a truck driver in a peer-to-peer in-class exercise.

2. **Enabling objectives** for our first terminal objective might be:
   - Given a role-play situation, the participant should be able to:
     — Smile at each customer
     — Answer questions displaying the three aspects of courtesy
     — Show sympathy by apologizing when closing a lane on a holiday weekend.

Exercise 3.4. Performance agreement.

The performance agreement principle is the relationship between objectives and evaluation tasks in three key areas: behaviors, conditions, and degree elements. Performance agreement is said to exist if an objective and evaluation task match in those three areas. Review these objectives and evaluation task examples and decide for yourself if they have performance agreement. Answer yes if they do, and no if they don't. The answers are provided at the end of the exercise. You may also want to review the section in the chapter on performance agreement if you are having trouble with the exercise. Note that some of the objectives will look familiar.

1. **Objective:** Given a list of email addresses, the Internet for Beginners participant will send an email message to all addresses without error.
   Evaluation task: Using this list of email addresses, send a message to each with your name and date.
   ☐ Yes   ☐ No

2. **Objective:** Provided with a stethoscope and blood pressure measuring equipment, the Nursing 304 student should be able to determine the blood pressure of five patients, as verified by the instructor.
   Evaluation task: Working with your instructor, determine if blood pressure readings are required of five patients, and if required, take and document the readings.
   ☐ Yes   ☐ No

3. **Objective:** Given participation in a role-play situation, the Effective Intercultural Communications student should be able to say "hello" and "good-bye" in at least two languages other than English.
   Evaluation task: You are one of 10 students on a work-study trip in Germany. You are staying in a remote village and you need to communicate the fact that you want to make a long distance call to a hotel clerk and a telephone operator in German.
   ☐ Yes   ☐ No

Answers: What did you decide? Question 1 has performance agreement. In question 2, the potential is there for the student to satisfy the objective, but it is also possible that the student might take fewer than five readings. Question 3 is a little tricky. You really have to wonder if "hello" and "good-bye" will be part of the interchange between the clerk and telephone operator. You must also hope that both the operator and the clerk speak different languages and that neither uses English. In this case, you cannot count on performance agreement.

4

Design: The Nine Events of Instruction

Chapter Objectives

At the conclusion of this chapter, you should be able to:

- describe the nine events of instruction
- provide examples of each of the nine events.

Lesson plans are an integral component of most instructional design projects. The single most important reason is that training often requires implementation of the same course numerous times. It is essential that each implementation of the course is done in the same way to ensure conformance to content and quality standards.

Over the years, numerous designs for lesson plans have evolved. While some designers may claim that certain plans have their roots planted firmly in a theoretical base, most lesson plans are the product of honest efforts at finding a way to offer facilitators some assistance in implementing a course.

The Theory Behind It

The work of Gagne, Briggs, and Wager (1988) is the best source for background information on lesson plan design. One significant aspect of learning theory they describe is the formalization of approaches in designing training. The theory supports the notion that learners are more likely to retain the concepts, skills, and procedures taught to them if they are presented in a way that enhances and supports the way the mind works.

Researchers have been studying how the brain works for years and especially how it retains information. For instructional designers the "how" is an important question. The very essence of the designer's role is making sure that learners leave with demonstrated mastery of objectives. The nine events of instruction join theory and practice in a way that can be utilized in most design situations.

Gagne (Gagne, Briggs, and Wager, 1988) built the nine events of instruction on the work of other theorists who studied the way humans process information and move it from sensing to processing to storage in short- or long-term memory. The nine steps in this process and each so-called event have an instructional design component that is critical in lesson plan design. The nine events have application in lesson plans in ways beyond that of lecture and other traditional delivery modalities. Every training intervention must be based on the way the learner processes information, or it just will not work. The nine events are universal in their importance to instructional design.

Here are the nine events of instruction in the author's and Gagne's terminology. In order to make the nine events more descriptive of their intent, the author has given them new, more literal titles. The terms in parenthesis are Gagne's original names for each event.

1. gaining attention
2. direction (stating objectives)
3. recall (recall of prerequisite information)
4. content (presentation of new material)
5. application—feedback level 1 (guided learning)
6. application—feedback level 2 (eliciting performance)
7. application—feedback level 3 (feedback)
8. evaluation (assessment)
9. closure (retention and transfer).

Nine Events Repackaged

It is also possible to take a more traditional approach to lesson design and arrange the nine events into three categories, which most people would view as a viable way to assemble a course. In that approach, the categories would follow this format:

A. Tell them what you are going to teach them.
   1. Gaining attention
   2. Direction
   3. Recall

B. Teach them
    4. Content
    5. Application—feedback level 1
    6. Application—feedback level 2
    7. Application—feedback level 3
    8. Evaluation

C. Tell them what you taught them.
    9. Closure (enhancing transfer).

Technology and the Nine Events

The nine events become even more important if designers are working on a project that is not a traditional facilitator-led course. Designers who use the nine events as the framework for this type of delivery system can be sure they will at least consider the ramifications of all these elements in their design.

It is important to remember that the nine events approach to lesson plans is not always appropriate. The technology involved may not permit its use. It takes a lot of work to build lesson plans this way. After designers use this approach for a while, they find that the thought process it stimulates becomes instinctive and that it helps them become better designers even if they never again build a lesson plan this way.

A Close Examination of the Nine Events

Descriptions of each of the nine events follow. Most of the events include an example that shows how to build a lesson plan using this approach. Exercises at the end of the chapter give you the chance to practice building your own lesson plan.

Gaining Attention

In the beginning of a course, it is necessary to help learners focus on the course. Sometimes gaining attention means setting a tone for the course, whereas other times it means turning off outside interference that is rumbling through a learner's mind. In all cases, the attention-gathering process needs to relate to the topic. A funny story or a joke is not a good attention-getting method as a rule because it can prove distracting, unless a facilitator is certain that it refers to the topic and presents it in a way that is not offensive to the learners.

Some of the methods for gaining attention that have proven effective include the following:

- playing video or audiotapes of one minute or less on the topic
- having a demonstration, such as modeling the task participants will learn in the course
- role-playing, particularly in affective and interpersonal domain objectives, such as sexual harassment and workplace violence.

Designers should not attempt to start a training program without knowing how the facilitators will gain participants' attention. The designers should let their imaginations go as they search for a way that will start their curricula off with an attention-getting bang.

Consider how a designer might use a video to gain participant's attention during a fictional safety course. (Note that this in no way is meant to be a real course. It is an example for lesson plans.) The course focuses on the increased risks of injury if proper safety procedures are not followed.

1. The designer says, "We are going to open our course with a short video highlighting the risks of injury that workers face in certain situations. The workers shown in the video are undoubtedly hard workers like all of us, but safety takes no holidays and this is a good example of what might happen."

2. Show the videotape—a one-minute depiction of an accident that injures several workers during routine work.

3. Ask participants what they observed. The designer reiterates the video's point about using proper equipment and procedures.

4. The designer closes by saying, "I think we can all agree that following safety procedures are necessities for every workers' well-being. None of us wants to be injured or killed on the job."

Direction

The presentation of objectives is a crucial factor in setting the framework for meeting the course objectives. Objectives set the destination so that learners will have a map that shows them where they're going.

Sometimes facilitators or designers say that they want learners to surmise the objectives or that they should be a surprise. Some facilitators or designers ask learners what they would like to learn in a course. If there are any examples of instances in which these methods are successful, they are rare indeed. As chapter 3 described, objectives are the nucleus of all other aspects of instructional design.

Designers should state their objectives in a way that works for their audience. At this stage, they have already completed the audience analysis, which provides the direction for designing the objectives.

For the worker's safety lesson the designer needs to set the direction for the participants early in the course, just as any designer would with any project. Stating the objectives in the second event acts as a stabilizing force in your lesson plan. The designer would take the time to think through what it is he or she wants the learners to be able to do and what they should be able to do at the end of that session. Following is one approach the designer might take:

1. The designer might say something like the following: "The risks of injury on the job are a matter of life and death. They involve everyone of us."

2. Before you leave, you should be able to identify the potential risks of injury you face on the job.

3. You should be able to demonstrate how to conduct checks for unsafe conditions.

4. You should be able to describe how to report unsafe working conditions to a supervisor or union representative.

Recall

To set the context for the objectives, facilitators must prime learners for the new material that will follow the three warm-up elements—that is, gaining attention, direction, and recall. It often takes a little bit of information to get learners thinking about the course content and objectives.

In some cases, the recall session may end up being technical to ensure the facilitator that participants are ready to move to the new material. Other times, it may be no more than a simple question or discussion that builds the foundation for the information that follows.

One design necessity of this prerequisite element is for it to level the playing field for the facilitator. Depending on content and course design, participants who lack the necessary competencies need assistance. A simple solution that works with some designs is to provide a simple handout or give a brief review. A more thorough review may be necessary if there is a large gap in knowledge or enough of the participants are having problems with the prerequisites.

Designers need to think through this aspect of their design. Effective designs build in options for the facilitators that allow them to add information as necessary once they determine a group's level of competency. For example, they could prepare to give participants handouts with prerequisite content as well as to hold a group discussion that covers the content. The discussion would work well in affective and interpersonal domain objectives.

Facilitators who find that one or more of the participants appear to be struggling with the prerequisite information could distribute a basic handout to provide them with a reference for the rest of the module. However, facilitators should watch out for those overqualified in the class for this activity. They may bore some and enlighten others, who find it as stimulating as reading yesterday's paper for the second time.

Facilitators who determine that one or more of the participants is competent enough to assist them with the class should sign them up for that role. They could have those participants circulate through the room, answering questions as necessary.

A pretest for review is a sound design practice. Instructional designers who are unsure of their population's entry competencies should screen potential participants before they attend a course, not after they arrive and expect to participate.

Content

How content is presented will have more impact on learners than any other facet of the design. Implementation is about presenting new material in a way that ensures that learners meet objectives. Designers can be as creative as they wish just as long as they balance this creativity with what their analysis has told them about the learners.

Designers who are presenting highly technical training that resides predominately in the cognitive domain need to find the balance between mandated content and its numbing effect on the learners. They must find a way to make everything interesting. Their projects will all be different when it comes to content. They must use their imagination to its full advantage and choose presentation modalities that interest the learner and make the most of the resources available. Following is one example of how to do it, using mining as an example:

1. The instructor may say, "You know your job like the back of your hand, right? So tell me where the danger is in this picture?"

2. "All of the pictures you're about to see show areas in which there were unsafe working conditions. Some of the problems are more obvious than others. All of the accidents were preventable. These pictures are also in your handouts."

Application—Feedback Level 1

Instructional designers like to use interactivity when building a course. It is almost as if they have an overwhelming need to allow and encourage participation by learners. The very word *participant* must have evolved from the notion of participation. To be effective, interactivity should not be a question tossed out into the room and batted around until something emerges. Designers need to shape and build momentum to keep the learners engaged. Application—feedback is the point at which designers can give the facilitator and learner an opportunity to begin practicing skills or discussing concepts critical to meeting lesson objectives.

In this first level of application—feedback, it is essential that facilitator and learners share equally in the process. One excellent way to do this is to have a large group discussion that involves working though a problem or discussing a concept. It is important that the facilitator involve as many participants as possible in the discussion and draw in those who are holding back. Learners need to have a comfortable environment in which to ask questions. They also need to feel safe enough to experiment and ask a question that, in another environment, they may not ask for fear it would seem ridiculous.

Application—Feedback Level 2

Individual performance and practice in a safe environment are the main benefits of this event. Learners should now be able to test the waters of the new material. Generally, this portion of the training is built around small group activities. It is important that learners have an opportunity to both offer and receive information at this point.

Designers who want interactivity can make it happen during this stage. They should find ways to invite learners into the subject matter and also offer a low-level evaluation of the objective or objectives by both the facilitator and other learners. At this stage of the process, learners are largely on their own and receiving feedback from other learners and the facilitator.

By working in pairs or small groups, learners may ask questions of each other that they might not ask of a facilitator. Designers must provide an easy path from the small group to the facilitator so that learners who are unable to find an acceptable answer among themselves can go to the facilitator for answers and clarification as necessary.

Application—Feedback Level 3

It is really tough for people to make much progress with anything if they don't receive any information about how they are doing. This element serves as a learner's friend and partner in training. Avoiding this element produces weak training in both stand-up and technology-driven areas. No substitute exists for midcourse corrections in the learning process. A learner should not be allowed to get to the end of a training event without any information related to meeting the objectives.

First, designers must make sure through the objectives that each learner will get enough feedback about progress to allow correction of any uncertainty or error. A facilitator, another learner, or even a computer could deliver this information. The important thing is that it is delivered.

There are a many ways to provide this feedback, and each design's specific objective domains, time limitations, level of difficulty of content, learner variables, and possibly other factors will influence each designer's approach. One of the true tests of a good designer is how he or she determines the best feedback scheme for his or her project.

In the safety example, course participants can review diagrams of their work areas to identify danger spots. A course like this demonstrates how important it is that learners meet objectives. An uncorrected mistake at this point may never get corrected and could eventually have life-threatening repercussions for the learner if an accident occurred.

Evaluation

If evaluation is one of the parents of instructional design, then evaluating performance is the first cousin. No learner should leave a training course without passing through an evaluation. This doesn't always mean a test or other formal evaluation, it is usually just a check-off that ensures that the learner has met the objectives. But every objective has to be evaluated, or it isn't worth having as an objective. This is the basis of the performance agreement principle. Objectives have to match evaluation tasks, and it is tough to match these two if one is missing.

Evaluation needs to be a step above just providing feedback to the learner. It is easy to deliver the evaluation in designs that include a formal evaluation, such as a final test or certification exam. Designers will need to find other ways of providing this feedback if they do not plan on offering an exam. For example, for a training program for a sales staff, designers might have a learner simulate closing a sale with a client. They can determine any remaining rough spots and provide the learner with any additional assistance needed to meet the project objectives.

There are several ways that designers could create the final evaluation for the safety class. One way is for learners to describe to all members of the class the risks in their jobs and present a safety plan to reduce them. This provides one learner with an evaluation and the other learners with ideas that had not been presented before. Most important, the facilitator has the opportunity to comment on the learner's progress and correct any problems that remain.

Closure

During closure, instructional designers need to review the objectives and provide a recap for learners. It is important that learners appreciate the progress they have made and realize that they have met the objectives presented to them at the beginning of the course. The satisfaction of charting progress cannot be overstated. To accomplish these ends, designers have to provide the following during closure:

- **Information about any course elements that follow:** Those elements might be the next course in a series or an optional add-on that is being offered. It is vital that the design provide a path to anything that follows. This path is not just for continuity, although it does provide that assistance, but also for prerequisite information so that learners know what to expect next. If they need to prepare any materials or read anything before attending the next course, they have the necessary information to do that.

- **Generalizing information about the knowledge, skills, or abilities provided in the course.** If the content deals with learning to use a two-quart pot for boiling potatoes, the facilitator might generalize by pointing out that the pot also works for making soup or by explaining two different ways to cook using the same pan. To take another example, in designing a course for attorneys about the communication skills for presenting opening arguments, a designer might generalize by showing that attorneys can also use that skill in closing arguments. At a communications level, only the words change, not the process of presenting.

- **Synthesizing, or finding ways to change the context of the learners' KSAs (knowledge, skills, and abilities):** This skill is to help learners find application of the objectives in a different frame of reference. In the pot example, synthesizing would mean using the pot for catching rainwater. In the attorney communications example, it might mean using that communications skill to argue for a refund at a department store. Synthesizing is important in expanding the dimension of the objectives. Once designers have moved the learner to the target objectives, they can really expand the value of the course.

In the safety example, learners might generalize by encouraging other staff members to look at photographs for dangers in their work areas and at home. The skill has not changed, but it is being generalized to include other areas where workers might confront safety issues. Changing the context of the objectives in this course might mean using a map of the learner's house and expanding it to include other danger zones. This is really using ISD to maximize the impact of the course.

Elimination of Events

Occasionally, designers choose to eliminate events. Sometimes there just isn't enough time for them to go through all of them. Other times nine events may be too complex for a particular project. When designing CBT or multimedia, it can be difficult to design the necessary feedback and interaction steps. Designers may then decide that they can reduce the nine events to seven or fewer events. Usually guided learning, eliciting performance, and feedback suffer the most in this environment.

Designers should be sure at least to consider all nine events when designing their course. Without this kind of guide for designing their lessons, they are likely to have an outline of the content and an instructional design with no structure, which is the cardinal sin of instructional design.

In Conclusion

This chapter finished the exploration of design. It describes the nine events of instruction, which are steps that guide instructors through the design of an effective lesson plan. The chapter also explained instances in which it may be necessary to reorder or eliminate some steps.

Putting What You Have Learned Into Action

Now, let's work through some exercises to build your confidence and start you on the road to designing a project of your own. The exercises that follow cover these topics, which together are the nine events of instruction of a lesson plan:

- ✓ Gaining attention
- ✓ Direction

✓ Recall

✓ Content

✓ Application—Feedback 1

✓ Application—Feedback 2

✓ Application—Feedback 3

✓ Evaluation

✓ Closure

Each exercise will give you an opportunity to practice the individual elements. If you are working on a project, use content from it as answers for the exercises. Otherwise, just use good ideas that will work for a number of different situations.

Exercise 4.1. Poison prevention course, part 7. Gaining attention.

Designers must gain attention at the start of their lessons, or they are likely not to hold the learners' attention at all. This exercise gives you a chance to be the designer in the poison prevention course. You are introducing a video to get students' attention. After you've completed the following exercise, adapt it to one of your own.

1. Convey this message in your own words: "We are going to open our course with a short video highlighting the dangers that poisons present in our homes and offices. The Jones family is probably like your family in many ways."

2. You would then show a one-minute video that depicts an accident with poison that injures a household pet in a typical home.

3. In your own words, ask participants what they observed. If the video did not mention **prevention,** be sure to introduce the concept.

4. Communicate the following message using your own words: "I think we can all agree that the safe handling of poisons is a necessity if we have small children or pets. None of us wants to be in the position of the Jones family."

Exercise 4.2. Gaining attention.

Now, it is your turn to apply this exercise to your course. Think of several ways to gain the attention of learners at the beginning of a lesson. Don't be afraid to be creative or to do something a little unusual. For example:

1. Show a picture or short video segment that highlights an important concept or skill that relates to the lesson objectives. Offer a quote, site a statistic, or tell a story to gain attention. Anything that helps a learner leave all the outside noise at the door is a powerful way to gain attention.

2. _____
   _____

3. _____
   _____

4. _____
   _____

5. _____
   _____

Exercise 4.3. Poison prevention course, part 8. Direction.

Using the poison prevention course as a model for writing objectives, set the direction for this group early in the course. The audience for the course is primarily adults, though some teenagers and younger children will also attend.

In any project, a statement of the objectives in the second event acts as a stabilizing force in your lesson plan. Take the time to think through what you want learners to be able to do after they complete the lesson and what you will tell them they will be able to do at the end of the session. The objectives for the poison prevention course will look like those that follow. Imagine your own project here and how you might do it differently.

1. An instructor might say, "The topic of poisoning prevention is much too important an issue to address simply by passing out a brochure or having you listen to several speakers."

2. "Before you leave, you should be able to demonstrate how to safely store containers holding potentially poisonous substances that may exist in your home."

3. "You should be able to identify several symptoms of poisoning in small children or animals."

4. "You should also be able to participate in a mock phone call to a poison prevention hot line during which you seek information on a specific chemical or product."

Exercise 4.4. Direction.

Stating objectives to learners paves the way for them to see the direction they are heading. Make sure they know where they are going. Objectives can be stated in both formal and informal language depending on the designer's intent and audience. The important thing is that the participants know what they are going to be doing with their time. Take a few moments and try several different approaches to presenting lesson objectives to learners in your course. The first one is done for you.

1. At the end of this morning's orientation, you should be able to describe at least three types of benefits available to you as a result of working for our organization. (employee orientation example)

2. _____
   _____

3. _____
   _____

4. _____
   _____

5. _____
   _____

Exercise 4.5. Recall.

It is vitally important that learners have an opportunity to recall concepts they learned previously if those concepts are necessary for learning new ones in a lesson. It is usually pretty easy to set the groundwork for new materials, but it is very important to do so as a design consideration. In this element, be sure to prepare learners for what follows by providing a chance for them to learn any prerequisite concepts, especially as stated in the design plan.

(continued on next page)

Exercise 4.5. Recall. *(continued)*

Write several ways to assist learners in recalling concepts that are a basis for presenting new material. The first one has been done for you. It is for a course with the prerequisite that learners have the ability to add and subtract numbers. Do the others using your course if it requires them to recall previously learned concepts. Otherwise, use your imagination to create questions on a topic of your choice.

1. For a simple adult course in reconciling a checkbook, you might want learners to practice simple addition and subtraction problems.

2. _____
   _____

3. _____
   _____

4. _____
   _____

5. _____
   _____

Exercise 4.6. Poison prevention course, part 9. Content.

Designers can present content creatively as long as it fits what their analysis told them about the learners, so the learners will respond to it. Consider the following way an instructor might present content from the poison prevention course:

1. The instructor may say, "One of the most important aspects of poison prevention is knowing which chemicals and products are dangerous. Many pet owners don't know that chocolate is a deadly poison to dogs. And large quantities of most of the common items in our home that we think are safe actually have the potential to be life threatening. Remember that you can drown in too much water, a basic chemical that's necessary for life."

2. "In our first slide, you see a list of common products in our homes that may cause a poisoning hazard." (Show slide 1-1.)

3. "This information is also in your workbooks on page 17 for future reference." (Hold up a copy of the workbook.)

Exercise 4.7. Content.

This is where you place the bulk of your subject matter information. Support your content with a variety of implementation styles. Support as many different learning styles as possible. Be sure to mix visual information with the verbal presentation if you are using a facilitator-led style. In technology-facilitated courses, be sure the content is not just presented as if a participant is reading a book or looking at overheads. Make it interactive! Think of several ways you can present content to keep learners on the edge of their seats. Write down at least two different ways to keep learners interested while presenting content. The first one has been done for you.

1. Use overheads with content clearly presented in typeface of at least 18-point fonts.

2. _____
   _____

3. _____
   _____

Exercise 4.8. Application—feedback 1.

This is the first opportunity for learners to practice their new skills and receive feedback. Application—feedback 1 is the point at which designers can give the facilitator and learner an opportunity to begin practicing skills or discussing concepts critical to meeting lesson objectives.

Write several ways in which to design the first level of the application—feedback events for your course. The first one has been done for you.

1. Hold a class discussion and work through a problem on the flip chart.

2. _____
   _____

3. _____
   _____

4. _____
   _____

5. _____
   _____

Exercise 4.9. Application—feedback level 2.

Individual performance and practice in a safe environment are the main benefits of this event. Sketch out several different ways to design this element for your course. The first one has been done for you.

1. Pair off learners and have them work through an exercise on the topic. Have the facilitator move from group to group to make sure participants answer the questions.

2. _____
   _____

3. _____
   _____

4. _____
   _____

5. _____
   _____

Exercise 4.10. Application—feedback level 3.

The type of feedback a designer creates varies with each design's specific objective domains, time limitations, level of difficulty of content, learner variables, and possibly other factors. Write several different ways to provide a method for learner application and feedback in this element for your course.

1. Have each learner work through an exercise individually and then compare answers with a partner. Be sure to provide a range of acceptable answers to each pairing to ensure accuracy. Also, have the facilitator check each learner's work.

2. _____
   _____

3. _____
   _____

4. _____
   _____

5. _____
   _____

Exercise 4.11. Poison prevention course, part 10. Evaluation.

One of the best ways to evaluate each learner would be to have each one present his or her final poison prevention plan to the group and solicit comments. This method provides an evaluation for the learner—from all the learners and the facilitator—and gives the other learners a chance to hear new ideas. It also gives the facilitator an opportunity to comment on the learner's progress and correct any problems that remain. Consider what a facilitator might look for in a presentation.

Exercise 4.12. Evaluation.

No learner should leave a training course without passing through an evaluation. It is one way to ensure that the learner has met the objectives. List different ways to evaluate a lesson in your course. The first one has been done for you.

1. A quiz or test

2. _____
    _____

3. _____
    _____

4. _____
    _____

5. _____
    _____

Exercise 4.13. Poison prevention course, part 11. Closure.

In the poison prevention course, learners might generalize by encouraging friends and family members to draw a poison prevention map of their workplace or to draw one for a relative or a friend. This exercise generalizes the use of the mapping for poison prevention to include other locations using the same process.

Exercise 4.13. Closure.

Closure—a review of objectives and recap for learners—gives learners an opportunity to appreciate the progress they have made and a chance to realize that they have met the objectives. List different ways to bring closure to a lesson in your course. The first one has been done for you.

1. Give several examples of the new skill or concept in a different context than presented in the lesson. For example, addition and subtraction can be used to reconcile a checkbook and construct a family budget.

2. _____
   _____

3. _____
   _____

4. _____
   _____

5. _____
   _____

Reference

Gagne, Robert M., Leslie J. Briggs, and Walter W. Wager. (1988). *Principles of Instructional Design* (3d edition). Orlando: Holt, Rinehart, and Winston.

5

Development

Chapter Objectives

At the conclusion of this chapter, you should be able to:

- define the development phase of ISD
- list several aspects of development that require reviewing when developing materials
- give several reasons why pilot testing is essential when designing a curriculum
- describe a typical train-the-trainer scenario.

The **development phase** of ISD is the period that connects the design process with the implementation of a project. Plans and prototypes move to realization as the designer moves materials to a final draft stage. Additionally, programmers code technology-based projects, and graphic artists produce artwork.

As the buffer between design and implementation, development necessitates that the instructional designer carefully monitor the process elements. It can be exciting for instructional designers to work with a variety of different professionals, but it can also be hectic. Careful communication at this point pays dividends later.

One of the most rewarding aspects of the development phase for instructional designers is that they get to see all of the design plans coming to life. Manuals, videos, Webpages, and a hundred different tangible deliverables finally take shape. There is usually a collective sigh of relief once this happens, and it is easy to see why.

The development phase allows designers to put the finishing touches on the observable deliverables for a project. It is also the best opportunity to do pilot testing before a project goes into implementation.

Look and Feel

Development presents many opportunities to make mistakes in training design and production. Everyone has opinions about the way materials should appear, and it can sometimes be hard to get general agreement about even the simplest things. Designers play an important role in finding consensus and working with all elements of a project.

The process of moving from draft materials to a nearly final product is crucial to a project's success. Designers need to address any number of issues in order to ensure that the materials are satisfactory. Generally, they need to consider the following aspects of development when working on materials production:

- **Cost:** Designers must be sure they know what products are going to cost and that they stay on budget.

- **Deadlines:** They must set firm deadlines for production of materials and require that vendors stick to the deadlines.

- **Written agreements:** They must have everything in writing concerning paper, color, size, quantity, fonts, and other variables in their materials.

- **Samples:** They must always check a sample of the materials before the production begins.

- **Final approval:** They must be sure to approve final copy of materials, not taking anyone's word for anything.

- **Pilot test:** Before producing the final materials, they must conduct pilot tests or have a review by stakeholders in the process, or do both. A pilot test evaluates the entire design, not just materials.

Pilot Testing

The chance to evaluate a project before it goes into full implementation is a key component of the development stage. The theory for instructional design is the same as that for a play: Both need rehearsals. It takes time to get all the bugs out of the implementation materials and lesson plans.

It is logical to pilot test before designers start producing final materials and begin the process of delivering their course. Some designers include pilot testing in the implementation phase, rather than in development, and that is fine. It is more important to test a project before finalizing deliverables than it is to worry about whether testing falls in the development or implementation phases.

Companies often view a pilot test, or preimplementation practice session, as a luxury. Even if it is a luxury, that doesn't mean designers cannot expose their project to some scrutiny before moving it into implementation. At the very least, it can be useful to do a dry run with a colleague or a friend. Here are some things that designers should look for in a pilot test. If they detect any problems, they should correct them before finalizing that aspect of the program.

- Does the lesson plan work?
- Are the directions to the facilitator clear and concise?
- Are the facilitator's materials appropriate and thorough enough?
- Are the learner's materials appropriate and thorough enough?
- Are the support materials (slides, overheads, handouts, and the like) what you expected?
- Does the timing of each of the segments match your estimates?
- Are the technology components (audio, video, computers, and so forth) appropriate?
- Do the instructional methods work as planned?
- What does not work the way you thought it should?
- What needs to be changed?

During the review, designers should look for anything that doesn't seem to fit. Sometimes designers' instinct brings to their attention problems that may not be obvious to the subject matter experts or the client. It is this sixth sense about design that makes the role of the instructional designer so important.

Another way to discover any problems is with a train-the-trainer program.

Train the Trainer

Trainers who will deliver a course find it helpful to see it and practice giving it before they implement it. A good model for designers to use is, See one, do one. In other words, have the potential trainers watch someone else conduct the course and then practice implementing it themselves. A train-the-trainer program often requires new facilitators to be participants in the course the first time through. This participation gives them the advantage of seeing the course from the perspectives of both the participant and the facilitator. This type of train-the-trainer course usually lasts at least twice as long as the course itself to provide the necessary opportunities for new facilitators to practice implementing the course. It is possible to shorten the time by having facilitators practice only key elements of the new course. Variations include having facilitators just practice specific sections, typically those that are difficult or require knowledge that may be unfamiliar to them.

One trap to be careful of in these train-the-trainer sessions is that some participants, frequently subject matter experts or new facilitators, may second guess every vowel and consonant in the project. It sometimes takes a thick skin for designers to keep their cool. One good designer's tool is patience. The key word here is **listen.** Nothing is ever gained by closing off contact with the key stakeholders in the process. As painful as it sometimes becomes, it is possible for a designer to become blinded by one or more elements of the design.

Putting What You Have Learned Into Action

The exercises that follow give you an opportunity to review the development phase of ISD.

Exercise 5.1. Poison prevention course, part 12. Train the trainer.

A good train-the-trainer (TTT) program is essential to most training programs that two or more facilitators will implement in more than one place. Sketching out the process is a key instructional design task. The nine events of instruction process is a great model to follow in designing a TTT program for a new course. Consider this example.

It is necessary to provide a train-the-trainer course for all facilitators for the poison prevention course. It has been decided that there are 15 likely sites for implementation and that it is possible that there will be one facilitator for each site. The hope is that only one TTT program will be necessary since the locations are within an hour of each other and a central site can be used. Prerequisites for being a facilitator are part of the design plan, so choosing them should be pretty easy. During the three-hour TTT program, the designers will assist in providing feedback to the new facilitators. Each new facilitator will have an opportunity to practice each section of the course with other participants serving as the audience.

Exercise 5.2. Train the trainer.

Using the description in exercise 5.1, answer the following questions about how you would design a TTT program for your course. (More in-depth descriptions of lesson plans and design plans appear later in the book.)

1. Number of facilitators to train on the new project?
2. Can they all be trained in the same place at the same time?
3. Do they need to have a separate lesson plan for implementation?
4. Are there any prerequisites for being a facilitator (see also your design plan for facilitator prerequisites)?
5. How long will the TTT need to take? (often at least twice the length of the course)
6. Will each facilitator have an opportunity to facilitate all or part of the course?
7. How will feedback be provided to each facilitator?

Exercise 5.3. Pilot testing.

Development tasks focus on the course design and its effectiveness in implementation. In our poison prevention example, a pilot testing session would need to evaluate several different elements of the design plan. Be sure to consider every aspect of a project in order to ensure a balanced evaluation. In this exercise you will consider a number of different aspects of a project. Answer the following questions for your course. Add or otherwise modify this list as necessary for your course.

1. Does the lesson plan work?
2. Are the directions to the facilitator clear and concise?
3. Are the facilitator's materials appropriate and thorough enough?
4. Are the learners' materials appropriate and thorough enough?
5. Are the support materials (slides, overheads, handouts, and the like) what you expected?
6. Does the timing of each of the segments match your estimates?
7. Are the technology components (audio, video, computers, and so forth) appropriate?
8. Do the instructional methods work as planned?
9. What does not work the way you thought it should?
10. What needs to be changed?

6

Implementation

Chapter Objectives

At the conclusion of this chapter, you should be able to:

- explain the implementation phase of the ISD process
- explain Donald Kirkpatrick's levels one and two
- review the evaluation tasks associated with implementation.

Implementation is the ISD element that most nondesigners consider training and education. It is the time when learners sit in the classroom or in front of a computer for an online course. This phase connects the provider with the end user of the instruction. It is the most recognizable element of the ISD process.

It is an axiom in project management that you are never more than 90 percent complete on any job you are working on. It is the same with instructional design projects. It is time to move on to implementation if a designer has the basics covered, the pilot testing has gone well, and the designer has made the changes. Waiting for that next 10 percent improvement might take longer than the total time allocated for the project.

Not every designer implements the curricula he or she designs. In some cases, a designer may never actually teach the course or be part of a learning technology solution. Designers who do not teach are not necessarily following a faulty line of reasoning. In fact, it is probably a good idea. Designers who are also facilitators have a tendency to believe that they can improvise a fix for missing or faulty design elements on the spot. This is usually not the case. The ability to make alternations on the fly is normally the domain of the designer. Facilitators are not always as experienced or capable of making a faulty lesson plan work as designers might want them to be. Nothing should be left to chance, especially if it allows a design to suffer in the hands of an inexperienced facilitator.

The evaluation of the implementation process must include an evaluation of learners' impressions of the training (that is, Donald Kirkpatrick's level one) and the validation of objectives being met by learners (that is, Kirkpatrick's level two).

Kirkpatrick's Levels of Evaluation

Donald Kirkpatrick (1998) has broken evaluation into four levels that are easy to understand. Each of these has specific qualities and fits distinctive needs. Although these levels are linear, designers do not have to use them in any specific order to achieve their evaluation objectives. The four levels of evaluation are as follows:

- level one, reaction
- level two, learning
- level three, behavior
- level four, return-on-investment.

This chapter includes descriptions of levels one and two, which are essential ingredients of evaluation during implementation. Descriptions of levels three and four appear in chapter seven, which covers the evaluation phase of ADDIE.

Reaction, Level One

Anyone who has ever completed an evaluation that asked for a reaction to a training course probably was responding to a level one evaluation. The most common evaluations at this level are smile sheets, which ask about likes and dislikes. Smile sheets are so common that some people use the term to refer to all evaluations at this level. Other level one evaluations are focus groups, which are held after training, and selective interviews in which people ask a sample of learners their opinions of training as they leave a program. The aim of each of these level one evaluations is to discover learners' reactions to the process. More than anything, level one evaluations provide instant quality control data. ASTD reports that between 72 and 89 percent of organizations use level one evaluations (Bassi and Van Buren, 1999).

A good strategy for level one evaluations is to determine learners' initial responses to the experience as they exit the training. The freshest and most accurate data for a level one evaluation comes at the immediate conclusion of the training. Every minute that elapses from the end of the training to the reaction from a participant adds to the potential that inaccurate data will be collected. After all, designers are looking for a reaction.

Typical questions include:

- Was your time well spent in this training?
- Would you recommend this course to a co-worker?
- What did you like best?
- What did you like least?
- Were the objectives made clear to you?
- Do you feel you were able to meet the objectives?
- Did you like the way the course was presented?
- Was the room comfortable?
- Is there anything you would like to tell us about the experience?

Behavior, Level Two

For instructional designers, evaluations at the learning level are tied directly to objectives. These are the evaluation tasks that designers develop to match their objectives. Surprisingly, only 29 to 32 percent of organizations use a level two evaluation (Bassi and Van Buren, 1999). This statistic indicates that less than a quarter of all training is evaluated in relationship to objectives, assuming there are any.

Performance agreement goes a long way to ensuring that objectives are correctly evaluated. Chapter 3 described the following objective:

> You have just entered the office of a major client. You have to make a case for buying your top-line product. It is important that you present at least three reasons why the client should purchase your product.

The designer would then match the key elements of behavior, condition, and degree in the objective and the evaluation task. Table 5 shows the key elements. The evaluation task column shows what Kirkpatrick calls level two evaluations.

Designers who follow the performance agreement principle of comparing the behavior and condition elements of both an objective and evaluation task will be accomplished level two designers.

Table 5. The performance agreement match.

	Objective	Evaluation Task
Behavior	. . . the learner . . . should be able to present . . . reasons why the client should purchase a specific product	. . . you present . . . reasons why the client should purchase your product
Condition	Given a realistic role-play situation with . . . learner playing the part of the salesperson . . .	You have just entered the office of a major client. You have to make a case for buying your top-line product.
Degree	. . . present three reasons . . .	. . . three reasons . . .

Other Elements of Evaluation

During implementation, other elements of evaluation that must be present are as follows:

- evaluation from the perspective of the facilitator
- evaluation of the materials or technology
- evaluation of the environment (room size, arrangement)
- continuity and conformity of implementation with the design plan.

These elements are independent of the level process and have the potential for providing data that suggest changes are necessary. Every aspect of the design is subject to further alteration once implemented. As noted earlier, designers should never consider a project more than 90 percent complete. This means they have a work in progress, not a project that has no hope of redemption. Careful evaluation will provide ample opportunities for tweaks during and after implementation.

Even perfectionists will relax knowing that everything is a work in progress, including content and materials. They may get the check in the mail for their work or be assigned to another project, but the designs they have worked on are still maturing.

In Conclusion

This chapter described the implementation phase, when participants encounter the instruction, and the importance of evaluation during this period. Readers learned about levels one and two of Kirkpatrick's levels of evaluation, which provide designers with information on participants' reactions to the training and on how well the learning meets the objectives.

Putting What You Have Learned Into Action

Now, let's work through some exercises to build your confidence and start you on the road to designing a project of your own. The exercises that follow cover these topics:

✓ Applying the elements of evaluation to implementation.

✓ Performing a level one evaluation.

✓ Performing a level two evaluation.

Exercise 6.1. Poison prevention course, part 13. Implementation.

Designers should always make sure their project is working the way they designed it. In the poison prevention course, for example, we are concerned about the participants' reactions to the course and materials. We must also be certain that participants can meet the objectives for the course. Use the following list to review all aspects of the poison prevention course:

1. evaluation of the learners' impressions of the training (Kirkpatrick's level one)
2. validation of objectives being met by learners (Kirkpatrick's level two)
3. evaluation from the facilitator's perspective
4. evaluation of the materials or technology, or both
5. evaluation of the environment (room size, arrangement, and the like)
6. evaluation of continuity and conformity of implementation with the design plan.

Exercise 6.2. Implementation.

Now use this list to evaluate the course you're implementing. Check your design by reviewing the following:

1. evaluation of the learners' impressions of the training (Kirkpatrick's level one)
2. validation of objectives being met by learners (Kirkpatrick's level two)
3. evaluation from the facilitator's perspective
4. evaluation of the materials or technology, or both
5. evaluation of the environment (room size, arrangement, and the like)
6. evaluation of continuity and conformity of implementation with the design plan.

Exercise 6.3. Poison prevention course, part 14. Level one, evaluation exercise.

There are many ways to express smile sheet questions. They may be as simple as, "What did you like best about the course?" and "Would you recommend this course to a friend?" Other common questions at this level concern participants' feelings about the facilitator and whether the room and other logistics worked for the course.

Consider these possible questions for the poison prevention course:

1. Was your time well spent on this course?
2. What one new fact did you learn about poison prevention from this course?
3. Did the facilitator seem qualified to teach the course?

Exercise 6.4. Level one, evaluation exercise.

Now it is your turn. What questions do you want to ask participants to help you gauge their reaction to your course? Prepare several level one evaluation questions for your design project.

1. _____
   _____

2. _____
   _____

3. _____
   _____

4. _____
   _____

5. _____
   _____

Exercise 6.5. Poison prevention course, part 15. Level two, evaluation exercise.

Level two evaluations are connected directly to the written objectives. Designers usually write both evaluations and objectives at the same time. The poison prevention course has the following objective:

Given handouts, a job aid, and the class discussion, the Poison Prevention in the Home participant should be able to create a plan to store poisons that removes any chance that children or pets can gain access to a poison.

What would the level two evaluation be for this objective? Written as if it would be given or read to the participant, it would be as follows:

Using the sample map, the handouts you have been given, and the course discussions, create a plan for your home that removes any chance that family or pets might gain access to poisons.

Exercise 6.6. Level two, evaluation exercise.

Now, write a level two evaluation for the following objective or for an objective from your course:

Given a copy of the morning paper, the Current Events for New Citizens participant will clip at least two articles concerning news in his or her neighborhood.

_____

_____

_____

_____

A level two evaluation might read like this:

Read through the copy of the *Daily Bugle* you have been given and find at least two articles that are written about the neighborhood you live in.

References

Bassi, Laurie J., and Mark E. Van Buren. (1999). *The ASTD State of the Industry Report*. Alexandria, VA: ASTD.

Kirkpatrick, Donald. (1998). *Evaluating Training Programs: The Four Levels* (2d edition). San Francisco: Berrett-Koehler.

7

Evaluation

Chapter Objectives

At the conclusion of this chapter, you should be able to:

- describe evaluation techniques for all five elements of the ADDIE model
- evaluate the four parts of an objective
- describe evaluation as it relates to the performance agreement principle
- list the four levels of evaluation, as described by Kirkpatrick
- design evaluation instruments for all four levels of evaluation.

Evaluating More Than Just Results

Evaluation is more than just a postcourse event. Evaluation takes place in every element of the ADDIE model. Designers even need to evaluate the evaluation process.

Evaluation of the design process is just as important as a review of the content, and it is an essential part of a design strategy. If the same course receives positive content evaluations but negative process evaluations that show the course is not running smoothly, there are probably design process problems with either the delivery system or the instructional methods and materials. Positive process evaluations but negative content evaluations from the same course point to such content problems as difficulty of objectives, performance agreement, and other subject matter related areas.

Evaluations during each of the other four ADDIE elements provide the quality control mechanism that ensure an honest and meaningful snapshot of both process and product. It is almost impossible for a project to be completed successfully without a comprehensive evaluation strategy that goes beyond looking at the issues associated with learners and facilitators; the process itself must be examined. Analysis, design, development, and implementation all have evaluation needs that designers should include in their projects.

Evaluation in the Analysis Phase

Evaluation in analysis centers on the notion that a project with a solid foundation should never stray too far from where it is designed to be. Even when issues arise that need serious attention, a designer's analysis, if done correctly, will provide the blueprint he or she needs to fine-tune problems later. This is not to say that an analysis stands forever, as an accurate analysis will tell a designer. The evaluation at this point is intended to just make sure that designers have a great starting point.

Following are some questions designers need to address during evaluation. The responses will lead them to the things they'll need to evaluate.

- Is this an issue or problem that can be completely fixed by training alone?

- Is this an issue or problem that can be improved by a training intervention?

- Have you gathered all the data (enough data) concerning:

  — Population

  — Subject matter

  — Organizational goals

  — Learner goals and needs

  — Logistics

  — Resources

  — Constraints

- Have you reviewed your analysis results with:

  — Stakeholders

  — Subject matter experts

  — Target population sample

  — Other designers

- Have you compared your findings against other internal or external benchmarks?

- Have you double checked all of the above?

Evaluation in the Design Phase

Design phase evaluation is critical to the success of a project. Designers will have little chance for success if they allow a flawed instructional design to move forward to development and implementation. Objectives, evaluation tasks, and all of the critical elements of course design take shape in the design phase, and they need to pass some level of evaluation. Evaluations here address problems early and save time and money as an end result.

The value of design phase evaluations is that it enables coordination of information among all those working on a project. For designers working on their own, it is important to have someone review their design phase work because it is easy for designers to lose focus when they become glued to the process. A quick evaluation of both product and process is an absolute necessity.

Information from even the best analysis can go astray in the hands of a technical writer or designer. A SME is the best resource to use to check that the content is correct and clear. A SME's review can prevent embarrassing errors from occurring when the course is rolled out.

Designers need to ensure that the following evaluations take place:

- review of all the design plan elements by the SMEs and at least one other designer
- review of all objectives and evaluation tasks by the SMEs and at least one other designer
- review of evaluation strategy and materials
- review of all draft participant materials
- review of all draft facilitator materials
- review of all draft media
- review of everything by the decision makers
- checkoff on everything.

Evaluating Design Elements

Evaluating Objectives

The first step in the process is to identify each component in the objective. Following the recommendations made in other chapters, designers should scrutinize the elements—audience, behavior, condition, and degree—and rate them from one to 10 on the basis of how well they are written. Two examples follow. The first objective is not written well, and the evaluation of it shows where the problems exist. The second objective is much better and reflects good instructional design practice.

The first objective says:

At the end of this course, the learner will know about radar.

The components are as follows:

- **audience:** the learner
- **behavior:** will know about radar
- **condition:** at the end of this course
- **degree:** not available.

Here is a suggested rating:

- five for the audience statement
- five for behavior
- three for condition.

The designer would then calculate the quality of the objective. First, he or she would add the ratings, for a total of 13, then divide by four to result in a number between one and 10. For this objective, the score is 3.25 out of a possible 10. It is not very good, but gives the idea.

The next objective uses language more successfully:

Given four hours in the classroom and two hands-on exercises, the Radar 101 participant should be able to describe without error the five basic operational modes for a model R768 radar unit.

- **audience:** the Radar 101 participant
- **behavior:** should be able to describe the five basic operational modes for a model R768 radar unit
- **condition:** given four hours in the classroom and two hands-on exercises
- **degree:** without error.

The audience rates a 10 because it is not possible to have more information unless you name the students individually. The behaviors are a 10 because the objective states very clearly what the participant is expected to do. The condition is a little weak because it could include materials, so give it an eight. The degree is clear enough to deserve a 10. The score on this objective is 9.5, much better than the first objective's 3.25.

This use of a one-to-10 rating system may appear subjective, but a system can be developed that will apply to different designs and provide great value to the evaluation process.

Degree of Difficulty of Objectives

The term **degree of difficulty** does not refer to how difficult objectives are to write, but to how difficult they are for the learner to meet. An evaluation is important no matter what complexity or age group a designer is preparing instruction for. There are several reasons designers are concerned about difficulty. First, the level of difficulty in a series of objectives ensures placement from easy to hard in the design. The level may not be obvious unless the designer rates the objectives. Second, designers need to be aware of difficulty to ensure themselves that they are challenging their learners at the level at which their analysis shows the learners can both absorb and synthesize. Third, if they are evaluating another project, they will need to make sure that the level and sequencing of objectives are consistent with the project's goals.

Designers use the verb in each behavior for rating the difficulty because it is the heart of the objective. The verb shows that the designer is asking a participant to do "something" and that something has a level of difficulty. Designers should rate the difficulty the same as they do the objectives, using a scale from one to 10. Consider, for example, ratings for the following action verbs:

- **List** is not very difficult, so it will be a three.
- **Apply** is more difficult and deserves a five.
- **Criticize** is a 10 because it is more difficult than the first two.

(These ratings are just an example because there are contexts in which a designer may classify **apply** or **criticize** as less difficult than **list.** Subtle differences between items, for example, may make it hard to list them in certain orders, a lesson may be so clear that it is easy to apply it, and the merits and demerits of certain items may be so obvious that criticism comes easily.)

If these three behavior verbs were in one module, a designer would want to order them from easy to hard. There are exceptions, such as when a designer wants to start with a more difficult concept or skill and then move to easier objectives. But use your design skills to write and sequence your objectives according to their level of difficulty.

Performance Agreement

Performance agreement is the relationship between behavior and condition elements in objectives and evaluation tasks. The link between the two is critical to ensuring that the performance stated in the objective is in agreement with the performance in the evaluation task.

Performance agreement is comparable to motion pictures in that one of the most important jobs on a movie set is that known as continuity. The person who handles continuity makes sure the filming matches the script and ensures that the sequence of the final product matches the script.

Similarly, the designer must make sure that objectives are written correctly and that the evaluation task supports the objective in behavior and degree. The designer facilitates this process by checking performance agreement.

Following is an example of an objective and its evaluation task:

- **Objective:** Given a car and a filling station, the Fueling the Car participant will fill the car without spilling any gas.

- **Evaluation task:** You have just stopped at a filling station. Fill the car completely without spilling any gas.

This example illustrates performance agreement, as table 6 shows. The behaviors, conditions, and evaluation task match.

Following is an example without performance agreement:

- **Objective:** An intern working with a doctor at the hospital in the Internal Medicine Rounds program should be able to perform CPR on a patient during a Code Blue emergency.

- **Evaluation task:** You have been performing rounds with your assigned doctor, and a Code Blue has just been called in the next room. The nurse calls out that it appears to be a heart attack. You and the lead physician hurry to the room and determine that it is in fact a patient with no pulse. The lead physician orders you to perform CPR while he finds the defibrillator. In 500 words describe how you would perform CPR.

Table 6. The performance agreement match, example 1.

	Objective	Evaluation Task
Behavior	will fill the car	fill the car
Condition	given a car and a filling station	You have just stopped at a filling station

Table 7. The performance agreement match, example 2.

	Objective	Evaluation Task
Behavior	perform CPR on a patient	describe how you would perform CPR
Condition	working with a doctor at the hospital	performing rounds with your assigned doctor

Here the behavior in the objective and the evaluation task do not agree, as table 7 shows.

The conditions match, but **performing** and **describing** are two vastly different behaviors. In this case the mismatch could prove life threatening.

To fix this missing agreement, the designer could either rewrite the objective so that the behavior says, "should be able to describe" or change the evaluation task to say, "perform CPR on the patient."

It is a good idea to check performance agreement for all of your objectives, even if the consequences are not life threatening.

Evaluation in the Development Phase

Evaluation is also important in this phase, when many critical decisions are made that can greatly affect the success of your project.

Designers must make sure their evaluation plan is ready for the pilot testing of the project. Issues that typically come up as they pilot test are segment timing, deficiencies in materials, lack of clarity in the course structure, and missing the target population. A dozen other minor things may arise as well.

Segment timing is sometimes the hardest task for a designer. Differences in facilitators, equipment, and materials affect timing. A designer should allow for the possibility that any variable may effect timing. It is usually a good design strategy to add extra time. It is also valuable to time several run-throughs of a segment and average the time for the design. It is not uncommon to find **deficiencies in materials** during pilot testing. These problems can range from typographic errors in the copy to offensive graphics or wording. Sometimes seemingly simple issues like having the materials in the right language come into play. Just when a designer thinks everything is under control, someone will notice a problem in the materials, like an error in the CEO's name. Designers should fix all errors.

Clarity in the structure of a course is essential if the course is to be effective. Designers do not devote weeks and months to preparing a course just to watch facilitators struggle with the flow of the course, or participants roll their eyes skyward. Pilot tests often reveal holes in the population analysis, indicating that it undershot or overshot the average learner. It is the designer's responsibility to adjust the population information and content to match the pilot test's findings.

Evaluation in the Implementation Phase

The traditional approach to evaluation during implementation is the use of smile sheets, which show the reaction or response of the learner to the experience. Although these evaluations are an important part of a great evaluation strategy, they are only one small percentage of what a designer needs to do. Evaluation in this phase needs to cover every aspect of the interaction between the product and the end user.

Table 8 shows some components of evaluations during the implementation phase from the perspective of various stakeholders.

Evaluation in the Evaluation Phase

Designers who have evaluated everything in the other four phases will probably find the evaluation phase is the easiest part of evaluation. Evaluation

Table 8. Components of evaluations.

Learner	Facilitator	Client	Instructional Designer
Reaction	Reaction	Reaction	Objectives
Accomplishment	Usefulness	Value	Performance agreement
Valuing	Content	Effectiveness	Content
Investment	Presentation		Quality
Reality	Process		Timing
	Reality		Participants, clients, and facilitators
			Reality

products that designers may complete during the evaluation phase include project-end reviews and program evaluations for grants. Each of these is important and requires designers to do some thoughtful retrospection of both process and product for the project.

Project-end reviews have two purposes. First, they look at how well the process worked in delivering the project. Designers should conduct these reviews whether they are working alone or have 30 staff members. To arrive at some objective data, it is important that each person involved reflect on what happened and share those observations with the other people involved. If the training was contentious, it is best for the people involved to gather the initial feedback anonymously because participants may not want to give honest evaluations if they fear reprisals for their answers. Later, the designer can bring everyone together and work through the problems. If the problems are not fixed at the evaluation stage, they are doomed to be repeated.

Grants usually require program evaluations because the groups that give money want to know what they got for it. These evaluations give designers an opportunity to highlight the best part of the project.

Evaluation data, when presented with graphs or other visual elements, make the case for success. Designers should review the objectives and course rationale and then ensure that the evaluation underscores the results that support those goals.

Kirkpatrick's Levels of Evaluation

This book has made clear the importance of including evaluation through all stages of design and implementation of training. Chapter 6 explained the first two levels of Kirkpatrick's four levels of evaluation. Level one is reaction, during which participants tell what they liked and disliked about the training program; and level two is learning, during which designers assess whether participants met the objectives. Levels three and four, behavior and return-on-investment, take place following training. Explanations of these levels follow.

Behavior, Level Three

Posttraining evaluation is a level three evaluation. The most important question it seeks to answer is, "Did the training stick?" How much of the training transferred from delivery to the workplace? Between 11 and 12 percent of training is evaluated for behavioral change (Bassi and Van Buren, 1999). This statistic means that one training project out of 10 has been evaluated for effectiveness.

There are a number of ways to do level three evaluations so that any designer can add this level to a tool kit. Surveys and observation are two powerful ways to evaluate at this level. The thing to remember about this level of evaluation is the behavior. Did the behavior move to the workplace? If designers' objectives are written well, they have half of what they need. The other half is to select a way to measure where participants start and where they are when designers measure long-term results.

Designers who are interested in seeing if participants can meet the training objectives will evaluate learning, whereas those who are interested in seeing if performance has improved will measure behavior. Both of these can be satisfied with evaluation.

For example, evaluations would differ for a course on the use of new software for entering orders in a retail sales environment. A designer is interested in finding out if the course had any impact. Accurate data are available on how long it took to complete a transaction before the training with both the new and old software. At regular intervals, the designer accumulates new data on how long it takes to complete a transaction and compares the numbers. The designer can easily see any difference in time to see if the training had any impact and how much of an impact.

Designers who want to find out how much of the training objectives learners can still meet can sample a representative number of participants using the formal evaluation task used during the course. They then compare the scores on an individual or group basis and do the math. This method will go a long way toward evaluating if the content, instructional, and delivery methods were the best choices for the project.

In situations in which the evaluation is not so simple (with soft-skills or affective domain courses, for example), designers can interview or survey participants and gauge the participants' opinion of their ability to still meet the objectives. If possible, designers can also retest a sampling of the participants.

There are three basic reasons why participants may lose the ability to meet objectives after the course, each of which tells the designer something important about the course. The reasons are as follows:

- **Participants never learned the skill or concept.** If participants never learned the content, the designer may have a breakdown in the level three evaluation of the course objectives. Having a large number of participants in this category usually points toward implementation and design errors. Designers must carefully evaluate the course design and pay special attention to the population information.

  It is possible that the facilitators who carried out the implementation may have done a poor job or didn't follow the lesson plan as provided. It might be that the participant prerequisites were ignored. It is also possible that the evaluation tasks were either ignored or compromised to the point that participants were never evaluated at all. The lack of an evaluation sets up a scenario in which neither participant nor facilitator can really tell if the objectives are being met.

Design flaws could be as simple as poor performance agreement or disregard for a lesson plan structure that supports acquisition of content. Motivation and attitude are also concerns when objectives are not being met across the sample participant pool.

- **The skill or concept was never retained.** Problems with retention may come from any number of issues. The most common problems are too much content in too short a time or a lack of any supportive materials or methods after the conclusion of the course. It is also possible that the content had no meaning or importance to the participant. Ownership of the content is important if participants are to retain information for any length of time. Ownership necessarily implies content and course design that allows that to happen.

- **The skill or concept was never used after the course.** Designers who determine that participants had no opportunity to use the skills or concepts sometimes face issues beyond their control. They may train 300 women and men to be motorcycle mechanics, but if nearly all of them end up in sales, the training will not stick. These kinds of issues are especially important in psychomotor and cognitive objective domains. Yes, people may be able to ride a bike after many years of no practice, but how many years of practice have they had to support those skills.

Return-on-Investment, Level Four

A level four evaluation is about results. What was accomplished? Did the training contribute to an organization's bottom line? Were the expected or promised results accomplished? This level of evaluation has also drawn more than a few skeptics because inflated claims of return-on-investment have sometimes entered into the process and driven many to question any "claimed" results.

Probably fewer than 3 percent of training is evaluated for results (Bassi and Van Buren, 1999). Make no mistake about it, figuring results can be a tricky and sometimes expensive undertaking. One reason for this is that the value of results can be both monetary and societal in nature. Although the impact on an organization can be figured with some degree of certainty, the impact on a community is tough to measure and is largely subjective in nature.

However, no one should discount the power that training can have for change in a community. The poison prevention course, for example, is community based, and the impact could be literally lifesaving, a true level four result.

In Conclusion

This chapter completes the description of the five elements of the ADDIE model. It showed that the final element, evaluation, must be an integral part of all the other elements. The chapter also concluded the description of Kirkpatrick's four levels of evaluation.

Putting What You Have Learned Into Action

Now, let's work through some exercises to build your confidence and start you on the road to designing a project of your own. The exercises that follow cover these topics:

- ✓ Performing a level three evaluation.
- ✓ Performing a level four evaluation.

Exercise 7.1. Poison prevention course, part 16. Level three, evaluation exercise.

Level three evaluations gauge behavioral changes. Sometimes designers implement the evaluation both before and after the training so they can accurately measure the change. In many cases, it is difficult to do a test before the course, but designers should take full advantage of the opportunity whenever they can.

For the poison prevention course, you can make judgments about a participants' ability to meet the objectives without a pretest. You will need to measure how well the training stayed with the participants by looking at what they did at regular intervals after the course. For the poison prevention course, you could simply call or mail a questionnaire to participants. What questions would you ask? They would include:

1. Have you taken action to ensure yourself that poisons are out of harm's way in your home?
2. Did you take an inventory of your home's poisons after the course?
3. Have you had need to use the Poison Prevention Hot Line since the course?

Exercise 7.2. Level three, evaluation exercise.

Now it is your turn. What questions do you want to ask participants in your course to help you assess changes in their behavior. Prepare several level three evaluation questions for your design project.

1. _____
   _____

2. _____
   _____

3. _____
   _____

4. _____
   _____

5. _____
   _____

Exercise 7.3. Poison prevention course, part 17. Level four, evaluation exercise.

Imagine you are the instructional designer for the poison prevention course. A sponsoring organization asked you to determine a general return-on-investment figure. You have the following information to work with.

- The course design and materials development cost $3,500.
- The train-the-trainer courses cost $150 each session for materials and other expenses. You have given six sessions.
- Materials for an average community session cost $300. You have given 15 sessions.
- The local hospital has estimated that it receives approximately 100 poisoning cases a year at its emergency room. Each visit averages $1,850.
- A national poison control association has estimated that effective community training efforts can cut poisoning cases by 5 percent to 10 percent a year.

What is the estimated return-on-investment (ROI) for this course using all of the above information?

(Answer: $3,500 plus $900 for train-the-trainer sessions, plus $4,500 in community sessions for a total of $8,900 invested in the course. Using the figures of 5 percent to 10 percent, the savings in hospital costs range from $9,250 to $18,500. The ROI is approximately $350 to $9,600 for the first year.)

References

Bassi, Laurie J., and Mark E. Van Buren. (1999). *The ASTD State of the Industry Report*. Alexandria, VA: ASTD.

Kirkpatrick, Donald. (1998). *Evaluating Training Programs: The Four Levels* (2d edition). San Francisco: Berrett-Koehler.

Section 3

THE BASICS OF THE DESIGN AND LESSON PLANS

8

Design Plan

Chapter Objectives

At the conclusion of this chapter, you should be able to:

- describe the elements of a design plan
- construct a design plan.

This chapter gives readers the opportunity to assemble one of the two major components of quality instructional design—the design plan. The design plan serves as the anchor for the entire instructional design process. Once readers have mastered the individual elements of a design plan, they have the skills necessary to develop one for any project they work on in the future. The poison prevention course provides readers with a model.

The Design Plan

The process of designing an instructional program goes beyond delivering the training. Although most observers consider implementation the most perceptible part of the process, it just touches the surface of the designer's work. Even a great musician rarely just picks up an instrument and plays a song well the first time. Musicians spend a great deal of time working so that the notes their audience's hear come to life. The concept is similar for a design project.

Most learners, and others outside the design process, see only the facilitator and the other learners. They are seldom aware of the hours, days, or months that went into the project from the design perspective. This is where a plan document comes into place. Before, during, and after the observable aspects of the training are implemented, the designer's work is documented in a package of design elements that outline the basics of the project from the ISD perspective.

A design plan is also the detailed explanation that every project should have to be complete. Designers who cannot answer all the questions raised in a design plan may need to spend more time reviewing each element in order to ensure that they have a well-designed project.

Following are some important elements to include in a design plan:

- rationale
- target population
- description
- objectives
- evaluation strategy
- participant prerequisites
- facilitator prerequisites
- deliverables.

A description of each of these elements follows. Designers may come up with other things that are important for their project, and they should add or subtract sections as their projects demand. However, it is best to include them all in order to ensure a complete design plan that will cover all the bases. For example, designers in the training or education department of an organization may feel that facilitator prerequisites are unnecessary because the facilitators are known, and so they may leave them out of the design plan. There is no right or wrong when if comes to what is included. The important point is that designers have a design plan and that it covers all of the elements necessary to fully explain the project.

Rationale

A **rationale** is the mission statement for the project. A designer who can capsulize his or her project into a short, tightly written narrative has several important pieces of information about the effort and can communicate them to others. First, that designer knows where the project is going. Second, the designer knows how to get there. And third, the designer knows why it is important to go there in the first place. The rationale is comparable to a lawyer's opening statement.

A typical rationale is several paragraphs to several pages long. It should not be a word longer than it needs to be or a word shorter than is necessary to make the case for the project. Designers have to make sure they have a mission statement mentality as they write the rationale. In other words, they should make their points as if they were writing a mission statement for the project. They should let the cerebral side of the designer in them come to the surface.

Several key questions need to be answered in a rationale including:

- What are the reasons for having the course?
- What population or populations does it serve?
- Who is sponsoring the course?
- What is unique about it?
- Why should anyone participate as a learner or sponsor?

A rationale for the model poison prevention course is worded like this:

Accidental poisonings in the home are a horrifying fact of life in too many families. All it takes to set the scene for this tragedy is for someone to have a short lapse of memory during which the person forgets to close a cabinet door or a container of prescription medication. Those openings can be invitations to a curious child. Accidental poisonings can be easily prevented by implementation of some simple steps. The Poison Prevention in the Home course is designed to provide a quick, powerful lesson in poison prevention for any concerned adult.

Sponsored by a national health-care provider, this course offers a unique method of identifying potential poisoning hazards. Participants draw a map of their residence and highlight the areas that represent poisoning hot spots. Participants make a list of poisons in that location and complete a plan of action for dealing with any hazards. Because poisonings do not always occur in conveniently marked locations around the house, the course employs a secondary strategy for identifying hazards not usually associated with a specific room. Participants then list these hazards and develop a strategy to address those poisons.

This course is implemented in less than 90 minutes, with actual course time set at 60 minutes. The additional 30 minutes are for housekeeping items and a question-and-answer session after the formal class. Anticipated class size is 25 or fewer for each offering. This size allows for participant interaction during the course.

Handouts, a videotape, and computer-based slides will be provided for each facilitator. A train-the-trainer session will be required for each facilitator before he or she will be certified to implement the course.

The target population for this course is adults with an interest in preventing poisoning in their homes.

Target Population

For the design and the learners to resonate together in a project, designers need to define the target population, or end user. The description does not have to be a long narrative, but it should cover all the bases. Although everyone involved in a project should be aware of its target population, people still make surprising assumptions about who will attend their courses. Some of these assumptions are so far removed from the true population of the course that if they are not corrected, the mistake could ruin any chance that a design could work. For a course in a technical area, for example, designers once assumed that their audience would include newly hired entry-level personnel as well as seasoned veteran technicians or supervisors. Unless these designers reined in the target population early in the process, they would have wasted valuable resources of time and money either by implementing the course to the wrong population or redesigning it at a point that required making major revisions of content and techniques. To avoid that lose-lose proposition, it is important to focus on the target population section of the design plan.

The target population statement must include those aspects of the population that can cause problems from a design perspective. Too much detail is clutter that should be avoided. It is not necessary to hinge design decisions on population elements like gender and age if they will not affect course content. Designers should just stick to the facts that illustrate the population and have the potential to cause them problems.

As designers begin to write the target population section of the design plan, they should close their eyes and picture the audience waiting for the course to begin. If they cannot give a detailed description of that group, they either have a design problem to solve or an open enrollment situation. Designers should picture a group of people slowly emerging from a dense fog and, as they get closer, begin to add details to what they are viewing. Then, they should write down what they see and add as much detail as the situation demands. In some instructional designs, the population overview can become complex. Following is a description of the target population of the poison prevention course:

> This population is largely adults with a high school education and an interest in preventing accidental poisoning in their homes. This group will be self-motivated to attend based on the marketing strategy employed by the course sponsor.

Description

This section of the design plan paints a picture of the project that describes the structure of the training. Common elements to consider for the course description are as follows:

- total course length
- module length (if appropriate)

- instructional method
- materials.

For the poison prevention model course, a description looks like this:

The poison prevention training is structured and lasts 60 minutes. Instructional methodologies employed include lecture, small group activities, and learner presentation and discussions. The room must be ADA compliant and have the capacity to provide computer projection. Recommended class size is under 25 unless an assistant is available.

Designers must make sure their course description provides enough detail to accurately depict the design of the project.

Objectives

The foundation and direction of the design plan are set under **objectives,** and everything else builds from them. All the terminal objectives go in this section. At times the number of objectives may be so large that a designer must list them in an appendix or elsewhere for easy reference. Large projects can easily have hundreds of objectives.

The poison prevention course has the following objective:

Given handouts, a job aid, and class discussion, the Poison Prevention in the Home participant should be able to create a plan to store poisons that removes any chance that children or pets can gain access to a poison.

Evaluation Strategy

In the **evaluation strategy** part of the design plan, designers explain their thoughts behind the evaluation plan; they do not give examples of evaluation tasks.

The evaluation strategy for the poison prevention course is rather simple. It depends on participants working with others in the class while the facilitator moves through the course checking on each participant. The description in the design plan might look like this:

This course will use a level two peer-to-peer evaluation strategy supported by a facilitator's observations. With an open enrollment participant group this large (25 or so), it is unrealistic to expect to implement a more formal evaluation strategy. Given the time limitations (one hour) and instructional methods, it is necessary to rely on peer interaction to provide the first evaluation and on the facilitator to provide secondary evaluative support. It is anticipated that participants should be able to meet the course objective evaluated with this strategy.

The evaluation will take place at the end of the course when each participant is expected to draw a map of his or her house and identify possible poison danger spots. Working with a peer, each participant will complete his or her map and show it to a partner. Each partner will offer advice and comments for improvement. The facilitator will answer questions as he or she visits each group.

Participants will complete a level one evaluation to measure their reactions to the course and the training room environment.

The design need not go further than this description to ensure that there is a thorough overview of the evaluation process.

Participant Prerequisites

It is an absolute necessity that participants meet any prerequisites for a course they are slated to attend. This gatekeeper process describes entry-level competencies that are necessary to prevent population mismatches in courses. The analysis element of the ADDIE model provides this information about what the prerequisites should be.

Designers have to accept the fact that their prerequisites are not always honored. It is not unusual to see an instructor provide training at a lower level to provide for the least common denominator in the target population.

Designers can use a tool known as **ranging** to widen the gate for a course without throwing the prerequisites away. When they apply ranging, they are setting the highest and lowest points of entry for participation in the course. They would specify these points in their design.

An example will illustrate how ranging works. Consider a designer who is working on a new word-processing program. An organization is standardizing its software and upgrading it at the same time. There are a number of objectives for the four-hour course, and most require prior knowledge of the software's previous version. The dilemma is that many people in the target population have no experience with the software because they have been using a different program in their department.

The designer realizes that the new software is not that much different from the software other departments have been using. For the training course, the designer decides to remove some of the more advanced features of the software and provide a general overview of the new software. The prerequisites for the course will state the following:

> Participants must have at least six months' experience with any word-processing software that includes mail-merge and label-making applications. Participants with less experience will be required to complete the Basic Features tutorial for the new software before attending the course.

Ranging lets designers create reasonable prerequisites for participants and still provide a path for the learners who cannot meet them. This example showed how ranging would accommodate low-prerequisite learners. Ranging also provides for overqualified learners.

In the software training example, a small group within the target population has learned the new software on its own. This group does not need the training but does need the certificate in order to qualify for an upgrade. Ranging can accommodate that population by adding the following sentence to the prerequisite description:

> Participants with prior experience on the software have the option of completing a short evaluation to receive the course certificate.

The design plan would state the following prerequisites for participants:

> Participants must have at least six months' experience with any word-processing software that includes mail-merge and label-making applications. Participants with less experience will be required to complete the Basic Features tutorial for the new software before attending the course. Participants with prior experience on the software have the option of completing a short evaluation to receive the course certificate.

Ranging works well in most situations. It should not be applied in projects that require a very high level of entrance competencies or prior certification. In these cases the level of skills necessary at entry are fixed by the demands of the course.

The poison prevention class would have a different type of participant prerequisites description than the software class. This class has open enrollment and, therefore, would not try to include or exclude people from participating. The description might say the following;

> Participants should have an interest in poison prevention and a willingness to participate in small group situations. The course will be delivered in English and requires some basic writing skills at the high school level.

Facilitator Prerequisites

Anyone who has ever attended a course that was facilitated by someone who did not have any substantial knowledge of the subject matter knows how important it is to ensure that facilitators meet certain specifications. These prerequisites allow designers to prepare lesson plans and other materials knowing that facilitators meet a necessary skill level. Designers who add this information to their design plan move their work up a notch in terms of design skills. The specification for the software class might state:

> The facilitator must have attended an advanced course in the software and received certification as a facilitator.

For the poison prevention course, the prerequisites for facilitators state:

The facilitator must have attended the four-hour train-the-trainer program sponsored by the course provider. Those unable to attend the train-the-trainer course may also qualify as a facilitator by assisting with at least four course presentations.

This example shows that ranging also works for facilitators. By providing an entryway for potential facilitators who did not attend the train-the-trainer program, the designer has provided a second path by which to meet the qualifications.

Deliverables

In the last section of the design plan, designers specify everything that will be delivered as part of the project. Deliverables are usually tangibles like analysis reports, draft materials, courses on software or other technologies, evaluation forms, and even the design plan itself.

The design plan would specify the following deliverables for the poison prevention course:

- analysis report
- design plan
- draft facilitator's guide
- draft participant handouts and information sheets
- draft evaluation instruments
- final camera-ready copies of all draft materials
- project evaluation.

In Conclusion

This chapter explained that the design plan is the detailed description of every aspect of a design project. Plans typically include each of the following elements:

- rationale
- target population
- description
- objectives
- evaluation strategy
- participant prerequisites

- facilitator prerequisites
- deliverables.

The chapter defined each of the elements and included examples of how a designer might explain each one in a plan.

Putting What You Have Learned Into Action

The exercises that follow give you an opportunity to review a completed design plan and complete one for your own course. They cover each topic in the design plan.

Exercise 8.1. Poison prevention course, part 18. Rationale.

This exercise shows a completed design plan for the course Poison Prevention in the Home. This plan may also serve as a template for design projects in any subject area you choose. Although the content may vary, the basics of great design plans never change. Consider how you will use this design plan.

Rationale

Accidental poisonings in the home are a horrifying fact of life in too many families. All it takes to set the scene for this tragedy is for someone to have a short lapse of memory during which the person forgets to close a cabinet door or a container of prescription medication. Those openings can be invitations to a curious child. Accidental poisonings can be easily prevented by implementation of some simple steps. The Poison Prevention in the Home course is designed to provide a quick, powerful lesson in poison prevention for any concerned adult.

Sponsored by a national health-care provider, this course offers a unique method of identifying potential poisoning hazards. Participants draw a map of their residence and highlight the areas that represent poisoning hot spots. Participants make a list of poisons in that location and complete a plan of action for dealing with any hazards. Because poisonings do not always occur in conveniently marked locations around the house, the course employs a secondary strategy for identifying hazards not usually associated with a specific room. Participants then list these hazards and develop a strategy to address those poisons.

(continued on next page)

Exercise 8.1. Poison prevention course, part 18. Rationale. *(continued)*

This course is implemented in less than 90 minutes, with actual course time set at 60 minutes. The additional 30 minutes are for housekeeping items and a question-and-answer session after the formal class. Anticipated class size is 25 or fewer for each offering. This size allows for participant interaction during the course.

Handouts, a videotape, and computer-based slides will be provided for each facilitator. A train-the-trainer session will be required for each facilitator before he or she will be certified to implement the course.

The target population for this course is adults with an interest in preventing poisoning in their homes.

Target Population

This population is largely adults with a high school education and an interest in preventing accidental poisoning in their homes. This group will be self-motivated to attend based on the marketing strategy employed by the course sponsor.

Course Description

The poison prevention training is structured and lasts 60 minutes. Instructional methodologies employed include lecture, small group activities, and learner presentation and discussions. The room must be ADA compliant and have the capacity to provide computer projection. Recommended class size is under 25 unless an assistant is available.

Objective

Given handouts, a job aid, and class discussion, the Poison Prevention in the Home participant should be able to create a plan to store poisons that removes any chance that children or pets can gain access to a poison.

Evaluation Strategy

This course will use a level two peer-to-peer evaluation strategy supported by a facilitator's observations. With an open enrollment participant group this large (25 or so), it is unrealistic to expect to implement a more formal evaluation strategy. Given the time limitations (one hour) and instructional methods, it is necessary to rely on peer interaction to provide the first evaluation and on the facilitator to provide secondary evaluative support. It is anticipated that participants should be able to meet the course objective evaluated with this strategy.

Participant Prerequisites

Participants should have an interest in poison prevention and a willingness to participate in small group situations. The course will be delivered in English and requires some basic writing skills at the high school level.

Facilitator Prerequisites

The facilitator must have attended the four-hour train-the-trainer program sponsored by the course provider. Those unable to attend the train-the-trainer course may also attend and assist in at least four course presentations as an assistant to qualify as a facilitator.

Deliverables

- analysis report
- design plan
- draft facilitator's guide
- draft participant handouts and information sheets
- draft evaluation instruments
- final camera-ready copies of all draft materials
- project evaluation.

Exercise 8.2. Design plan exercise.

For this exercise, use a course that you are designing or might be working on in the future. If you don't have anything in mind, you can use either the poison prevention model course or another topic that interests you. It works best if you stick with one topic for all of the exercises.

Rationale

- What are the reasons for having the course?

_____

_____

_____

(continued on next page)

Exercise 8.2. Design plan exercise. *(continued)*

- What population or populations does it serve?

_____

_____

_____

- Who is sponsoring the course?

_____

_____

_____

- What is unique about it?

_____

_____

_____

- Why should anyone participate as a learner or sponsor?

_____

_____

_____

Target Population

Okay, now take some time and think about your learners. Imagine them sitting in a room looking at you. Describe them in as much detail as is necessary to make the population come alive in your description.

_____

_____

_____

Description

Describe the course. Some questions to consider when writing a course design include the following:

- total course length
- module length
- instructional method
- materials
- specific logistical needs

_____

_____

_____

Objectives

What are the objectives for your course? Describe them using the A – B – C – D format.

- audience

_____

_____

_____

- behavior

_____

_____

_____

- condition

_____

_____

_____

- degree

_____

_____

_____

(continued on next page)

Exercise 8.2. Design plan exercise. *(continued)*

Evaluation Strategy

Write the evaluation strategy for your course describing all four levels of evaluation. The example is to get you started.

1. Evaluations will require participants to use the drill press successfully in the workshop environment. (level two example)

2. _____
   _____

3. _____
   _____

4. _____
   _____

Participant Prerequisites

What are the participant prerequisites for your course. The example is to get you started.

1. Must have passed high school algebra.

2. _____
   _____

3. _____
   _____

4. _____
   _____

Facilitator Prerequisites

Sketch out several facilitator prerequisites for your course. The example is to get your started.

1. Must have a high school diploma or GED

2. _____
   _____

3. _____
   _____

4. _____
   _____

Deliverables

What deliverables might be important for the course? Please add anything that might be missing.

1. materials

2. _____
   _____

3. _____
   _____

4. _____
   _____

9

Lesson Plan

Chapter Objectives

At the conclusion of this chapter, you should be able to:

- name the elements of a lesson plan
- construct a lesson plan.

This chapter gives readers the opportunity to complete the second of two important instructional design elements—the lesson plan. By working from the design plan they completed in the previous chapter, readers will be able to create a finished design project worthy of implementation. The exercises at the end of the chapter provide readers with a template from which to build their own lesson plan.

The Facilitator

No one likes to get lost while driving. In many people, getting lost evokes feelings of aggravation and stress, and those feelings are intensified if they are also late. Designers should keep this in mind when they are working on a training project. If they fail to offer facilitators all the information they need to implement the project, they will get lost. The stress associated with facilitating a misdirected training course can have disastrous effects on both the facilitator and the participants.

It is sometimes worse to get skimpy directions than none at all. Right now, a distressed trainer is sitting over coffee somewhere wondering how to deliver an eight-hour course from two pages of an outline.

The facilitator is as vital to the success of a design project as any other element. The more information designers can provide facilitators, the more likely they are to succeed. Lesson plans must be complete enough to allow anyone with the necessary subject matter experience to lead the course.

One of the first things designers need to consider as they approach the lesson plan stage of their design work is who their facilitators are. They should consider the following:

- Can they identify a range of experience within the potential facilitator's pool?

- Are there issues they need to address outside the normal curve, such as language or culture concerns? Will the facilitators require materials in a second language? Does the lesson plan allow facilitators to lead the course in a way that is culturally appropriate?

The information about the facilitators should appear in their design plan because it aids in the development of their lesson plan.

The Format

Every lesson plan needs to have a format that lends itself to making the implementation of the course as simple as possible. Designers need a consistent format if there will be a series of courses. Some stylistic elements that allow for an easy transition from one course to the next include the following:

- *Notations about wording:* The plan could provide information about what facilitators need to communicate but specify that they should put the information in their own words. The plan might say, for example: ***In your own words . . .***

In the next hour that we have together, we will learn about working in teams.

The suggested language should be styled so that it is easy for the facilitator to spot it on the page.

- *Action items:* Action items may be set in bold type to allow facilitators to see what they are expected to do next, as the following shows:

  Show slide # 78

  Start the video

- *The nine events of instruction:* Each of the nine events is covered in a separate section of the plan, and the titles of each get distinctive treatment. Together Gagne's nine events form the basis of the lesson plan. The events, which chapter 4 describes in detail, are as follows:

1. gaining attention
2. direction (stating objectives)
3. recall (recalling prerequisite information)
4. content (presentation of new material)
5. application—feedback level 1 (guided learning)
6. application—feedback level 2 (eliciting performance)
7. application—feedback level 3 (feedback)
8. evaluation (assessment)
9. closure (retention and transfer).

In the final plan, the name of each event appears in a box along with the suggested time for implementation, like that for "gaining attention." Designers may choose different labels for the sections, but whatever name they give, they should let facilitators know how long each one should take to implement.

Gaining Attention—5 minutes

This chapter contains a detailed exercise that covers the creation of a lesson plan and includes suggestions for success. As you answer the questions, you may consult the appendix for the completed lesson plan for the poison prevention course. The format for the poison prevention course begins with a checklist of activities that start 24 hours before the course and lead up to the beginning of the course. The plan goes on to detail the nine events of instruction section that contains the actual course. Designers who use a format with descriptive notes to facilitators make it much easier to obtain success with the course.

Putting What You Have Learned Into Action

Now, it's your turn to build a lesson plan. In this series of exercises, you have the option of using content for your own course, or you may use the subject matter from the poison prevention course. Either way, work through each exercise to build the lesson plan. If any of the elements presents a challenge for you, you may check the lesson plan in the appendix.

Exercise 9.1. Creating a lesson plan.

Element one: Gaining attention

Participants enter the training session with the outside world ringing in their ears. Write down several ways you can reduce that outside noise in your participants and prepare them to start the course. It is this first element that gets them to focus on the task ahead. Remember that this element should usually take no longer than two to three minutes. Following is one example to get you started.

1. Show a short video or use a projected visual to make a point related to the objectives for the course.

2. _____
_____
_____

3. _____
_____
_____

Element two: Direction

This element of a lesson plan tells participants what they will gain from their investment of time. It presents the objectives in a way that makes sense for the audience. You may state them as they appear in the design plan or in a different, more creative way. Think about the course you are designing and find the best way to tell participants what to expect. Try several different ways and see which one works best. Following is one example. Write at least two more.

1. Try using oddly shaped visuals of different parts of a process that when combined form a completed puzzle.

2. _____
_____
_____

3. _____
_____
_____

Element three: Recall

Before participants can start learning new content, they may need to recall concepts or skills they learned prior to the course. This may be information from last week, from last year, or from some other time. The recall element sets the stage for the new content to follow in the remaining nine events. As an example, in the poison prevention course, it is important that participants recall that many people are killed every year by preventable poisonings. This information appears in frame five of the lesson plan in the appendix and sets the stage for the presentation of the ways in which participants can prevent poisonings in their own homes. If participants do not recall this information, they may not make the connection between this course and their own lives.

For your course, what are the key elements that you need to make sure each participant knows in order to grasp the new content? Make a list and start to design your lesson plan recall element on the basis of that information. Following is one example. Write at least two more.

1. Practice basic math for objectives requiring that process.

2. _____
    _____
    _____

3. _____
    _____
    _____

Element four: Content

Content is the one element of the nine events with which everyone is familiar. It is the heart of the course, where most of the new information appears. Make sure the subject matter is presented in a manner that matches your design plan. Do not be surprised if you spend most of your time in this element because of the sheer volume of information to be presented. Proceed cautiously to ensure you have enough time to present everything you were expecting to include. Even the best instructional designers sometimes underestimate the time involved in presenting new content.

Map out your content and present it in a way that allows a facilitator to implement your course. Start from the foundation created in recall and work toward having your participants practice their new skills or concepts. Content appears in frames nine through 20 of the lesson plan in the appendix.

For your course, sketch out the ways you might present the new subject matter for a course. Following is one example. Write at least two more.

1. Demonstrate the proper way to access the new software on the network.

2. _____
    _____
    _____

(continued on next page)

Exercise 9.1. Creating a lesson plan. *(continued)*

Element four: Content *(continued)*

3. _____
   _____
   _____

Element five: Application—feedback level one

Now it is time for participants in your course to practice the skills or concepts they have just learned in the content element. You want this section to be guided instruction in which the facilitator works with the participants in joint activities, such as talking out a problem or working through a formula. In the poison prevention course, the participants and the facilitator look through a house to find potential trouble spots for poisoning, as shown in frame 21 of the lesson plan in the appendix.

For your course, sketch out a way for facilitator and participants to work jointly toward meeting one or more of the objectives. Following is one example. Write at least two more.

1. Have participants work through an exercise together using the flip chart.

2. _____
   _____
   _____

3. _____
   _____
   _____

Element six: Application—feedback level two

At this point, participants in a course get a chance to assume more responsibility for the learning process. Designers present activities that let them practice and ask questions in a safe environment. A great way for participants to have interaction and feedback at this level is for them to participate in activities in which they can work in small groups or pairs.

Describe what kind of activity you would like for your course. Be as creative as you can in describing a great activity. Review the poison prevention lesson plan in the appendix for ideas if necessary. Following is one example. Write at least two more.

1. Participants will be broken down into small groups and practice using the new phone system. Each group will be given several skills to practice.

2. _____
   _____
   _____

3. _____
   _____
   _____

Element seven: Application—feedback level three

Participants should now feel comfortable enough to ask any remaining questions and also to offer their ideas to other participants. Common exercises at this point include opportunities for participants to work one-on-one with others. It is critical in this element that the facilitator be looking over participants' shoulders to make sure that nothing has gotten lost between the content element and this one.

For your course, think of several different ways that you can provide participants with that one-on-one experience. It is possible even in large groups to allow this to happen. Be creative and start listing ways you can make this happen. Following is one idea. Come up with two more.

1. Each participant will be required to complete an exercise that involves all of the new skills incorporated in the lesson.

2. _____
   _____
   _____

3. _____
   _____
   _____

Element eight: Evaluation

This is your final gatekeeper function and provides either a formal or informal evaluation of the course. If you are required to evaluate with a formal test or quiz, you would place that element here. If you are doing a less formal evaluation, create a way to ensure mastery of the course objectives. Having one or more participants share their work with the group is a great way to evaluate performance. Make sure to provide opportunities for participants to ask questions. No one should leave with unanswered questions. Without this element, your course would be incomplete.

(continued on next page)

Exercise 9.1. Creating a lesson plan. *(continued)*

Element eight: Evaluation *(continued)*

For your course, take the time to write down your evaluation strategy. How are you going to evaluate participants' mastery of the program objectives? Following is one idea. Write at least two more.

1. Participants will be given a case study and asked to provide solutions for the problems presented in the scenario.

2. _____
   _____
   _____

3. _____
   _____
   _____

Element nine: Closure

The final element brings closure to the course. All of the questions should have been asked and participants should be able to answer for themselves if they can meet the objectives. If you can find a way to close with a story, or point learners to more information relating to the content, you will have created closure.

How will you close your course? Try several different approaches and see which one works the best.

1. Participants will be given several examples of how this process can be used in other contexts.

2. _____
   _____
   _____

3. _____
   _____
   _____

Exercise 9.2. Lesson plan template

Use the following template to help you design your own lesson plan. It includes the nine elements of the lesson plan in the order in which they appeared in exercise 9.1. You may insert your responses from that exercise here, or complete this template with different responses to create an all-new lesson plan that you can put to use.

Element one: Gaining attention

State how you will get your participants to focus on the course and the objectives. This is a very short introduction to your course.

_____

_____

_____

_____

_____

_____

_____

Element two: Direction

Present the objectives for the participants. You may do so formally, by actually stating the formal objectives, for example, or more conversationally by offering an example of what a participant should be able to do after the course.

_____

_____

_____

_____

_____

_____

_____

(continued on next page)

Exercise 9.2. Lesson plan template *(continued)*

Element three: Recall

Provide participants with any prerequisite information before you introduce the new content. This is a great place for you to review skills or concepts that are used as the foundation for the new material. What must participants know before they can take your course?

_____
_____
_____
_____
_____
_____
_____

Element four: Content

This is where you offer the new course content. It must appear in a way that permits facilitators to implement your course. What content will be in your course?

_____
_____
_____
_____
_____
_____
_____

Element five: Application—feedback level one

This is the first of three opportunities for participants to practice the new skills or knowledge contained in the course. Typically exercises at this level involve the facilitator and participants equally in the process. Large group activities are excellent at this point in the lesson plan. What exercises will facilitators and participants perform at this level?

_____
_____

_____

_____

_____

_____

Element six: Application—feedback level two

It is now time to shift the focus from the facilitator to the participant. Provide opportunities for practice and discussion that challenge participants. Small group activities work well in this element of your lesson plan. What activities will occur in your course?

_____

_____

_____

_____

_____

_____

Element seven: Application—feedback level three

At this element, participants take the lead and receive feedback at a one-on-one level. Feedback may come from another participant or from the facilitator. No participant should leave this element without knowing if he or she can meet the course objectives. What one-on-one activities will you plan for your course?

_____

_____

_____

_____

_____

_____

(continued on next page)

Exercise 9.2. Lesson plan template *(continued)*

Element eight: Evaluation

This is the gatekeeper function of your lesson plan. Evaluations may be formal, such as a quiz or test, or informal. Whichever they are, it is essential to ensure that each participant can meet the objectives. What types of evaluation will you include?

_____
_____
_____
_____
_____
_____
_____

Element nine: Closure

Now you need to bring closure to the lesson. Recap the objectives and offer any insights into the content that illustrate the usefulness of the information in a new or different way. Then, close the lesson and prepare for any lessons that may follow by building a bridge for the participants by mentioning how this lesson supports later lessons. How will you bring closure to your course?

_____
_____
_____
_____
_____
_____
_____

Section 4

TIPS FOR SUCCESS

10

Fine-Tuning Your Skills

Chapter Objectives

At the conclusion of this chapter, you should be able to describe the significance of each of the following instructional designer's tools:

- mental strategies
- avoidance of role conflict
- jargon control
- designer neutrality
- knowledge of designer types
- ability to deal with failure
- thinking big
- value neutrality.

Why Learn These Tools

Once a designer has learned to create a design plan and lesson plan, he or she knows most of what it takes to prepare and present a really great instructional package. However, being a great instructional designer involves knowing some of the rules of the road about working in the profession. These tools help designers go further in their careers by filling in some of the gaps that exist between preparing and presenting an instructional package and working in the profession. Think of these as fine-tuning a designer's skills, a bit of silent mentoring for the novice designer.

Mental Strategies

One of the most valuable skills any professional develops is the ability to master the processes necessary to that profession. It is that silent churning of the brain that calls forward every relevant bit of data that relates to the situation. Some call it a sixth sense; others, a second nature. Whatever its name, this background of information professionals have about their specific profession sets them apart from everyone else. It develops from both experience and formal instruction.

Police officers realize that one of the most valuable elements of that profession is the sixth sense they acquire about their surroundings after years of experience. That sense is vitally important and actually saves lives in certain situations.

Professionals in any field approach problems differently than the untrained. This is exactly what happens in every facet of life. The tow truck driver changes your tire in the time it would take you to open the trunk. The HVAC technician pushes one button and resets the fuse on the nonfunctioning heat pump that has been off for the last three cold nights.

Designers gain experience by working in the field with other professionals, just as professionals do in any other occupation. Some fortunate new designers are lucky enough to have mentors to guide them along. Even those who do not get that guidance can find ample opportunities to keep themselves sharp. The apprenticeship approach for designers usually encompasses watching, working, and waiting. The watching and working aspects are obvious, but the waiting may not be. Unless a designer is fortunate enough to work in an organization that is constantly providing opportunities for learning, designers in training spend most of their time waiting—waiting for something new to do, waiting for a new design challenge besides new employee orientation.

This waiting period proves most frustrating for new designers and may dull the design senses. But this is prime time for them to focus on the important mental strategies by thinking about them and reviewing them in books and articles. As designers develop a tool kit full of these strategies, they can add to their skills regardless of the opportunities for experiential growth.

An example of a mental strategy is the way a designer determines if a performance problem has a training solution. Many billions of dollars are wasted each year trying to remedy problems that cannot be fixed with training interventions. How frequently will time management training be used to solve the problem of poor working conditions or a terrible boss? Don't forget the cardinal rule of analysis from chapter 2: Make sure you have a training issue to solve before you provide a training solution.

Another example is designers' focus on objectives, not just on developing goals. A goal for a training course might be improving productivity. An objective might be that the participant should be able to complete all necessary company paperwork without error. See the difference? One turns the designer in the right direction, whereas the other gets you there.

Role Conflict

Instructional designers spend an inordinate amount of time attempting to point out to subject matter experts how much they can contribute to making a project work. It is sometimes difficult for nondesigners to accept that expertise in a content area that does not directly relate to curriculum design expertise.

Some of the hardest work for designers is convincing SMEs that they are better off leaving instructional design to the designers. Some would argue that this do-it-all attitude is more pronounced among SMEs in academics than in other professional fields. It is nonetheless a real issue for discussion in any training project.

The realization that they can't do it all requires the same mental process that most people go through when they try to fix a plumbing problem. Plumbers say their best service calls are from clients who have first tried to fix stopped-up sinks themselves. When the do-it-youselfers finally make the call, the problem is often worse than it was before the amateurs went to work, the plumbers make twice as much money as they would have at the first sign of trouble, and the homeowner is happy to pay every penny of it. Similarly, when people with no ISD backgrounds try to design training programs, their results are unworkable, and they usually end up calling in the training experts.

Designers may have to have several experiences with subject matter experts and even some unbelieving managers before they earn their respect and acceptance as part of the team. They should never take it personally if people question or challenge the value added by the ISD process. Every designer hears these questions. For each project, designers should develop a list of contributions that they will make. This list will help clarify responsibilities and will minimize the chance for misunderstandings later. Eventually the issue of role conflict becomes just another part of the process and is easily managed.

Jargon Control

Have you ever wondered why professionals feel the need to impress everyone with their ability to use big words and profession-related jargon? There should be a study to document every word, acronym, or unintelligible jargon used with the intent to impress or intimidate. Just think back to the last time your were subjected to jargon-speak, and you can understand how destructive it can be to the communications process unless everyone uses the same language. Can anyone explain why lawyers use the word **pro bono** instead of the word **free?**

Jargon like **the nine events of instruction** or **performance agreement** are important concepts in our profession. The terminology is so common to designers that they are apt to use it without being aware that it is special to the field. It is best not to use the terms with anyone who is not trained in ISD, including managers, clients, and the audience, at any function where the designer is the guest speaker. In short, designers must be careful to use professional jargon only when necessary and never outside the ISD family.

Designer Neutrality

Designer neutrality relates directly to issues of a political nature within an office. Curriculum designers will be put in numerous situations in which someone tries to force them to express an opinion in areas not related to design. These occurrences are most common when the clients are predominately internal. The office wars and personality conflicts that besiege every organization are not fertile grounds for designers. In other words, designers should not get involved in nondesign issues outside of their office or cubicle.

Neutrality is directly related to credibility. Designers may never get the respect of their client group if they wander too far away from designing. Designers who express an opinion about anything outside the sphere of the project may suggest to clients that they have other agendas or that they may be judgmental about them.

Subject matter is an especially dangerous area for designers to wander into. A designer can ruin a focus group or client meeting by expressing an opinion about a topic. Suppose a designer is in the middle of a meeting with an internal client on a proposed hot topic course. Several times the designer has commented on the subject matter in a way that suggests he or she has an opinion. The designer may later have to defend the design because someone thinks the content is slanted toward the designer's views. Rightly or wrongly, the designer is now part of the problem, and the designer's solutions may lack credibility no matter how well the training is designed.

Designers who are external to an organization can really get dragged through the mud. Office war participants love to have validation, and someone from the outside agreeing with them is usually all it takes to get something started. Just as with the internal client situations, designers should stick to design issues and avoid getting in the middle of office wars.

Types of Designers

Instructional designers can get involved in ISD in a number of different ways. It seems that almost every facet of training can take advantage of the benefits offered by this process. No matter which role a designer is in at the moment, there are probably a large number of people in the same position. Here are several of the roles that designers might play:

- **Designer and manager:** In this role, a designer also has the responsibility for managing all or a portion of a project or projects.
- **Full-time ISD manager:** An ISD manager does little or no design work and manages one or more projects.
- **Full-time designer:** This person does nothing but instructional design.
- **Designer and facilitator:** A designer both designs the course and is the facilitator.
- **Training staff:** A group of training professionals whose members do everything from design to facilitation.
- **Freelance consultant and designer:** This independent contractor works for a number of different employers.
- **Specialist in one or more ISD elements:** This designer concentrates on one element of the ADDIE model, usually analysis or evaluation.

All of these, and many more, represent the varied situations designers might find themselves in at any given point in their career. There are several reasons it is important to consider the different contexts in which instructional designers may work. First, novice designers should have a good grasp of the different possibilities they may face in the field. Second, there is no one right or wrong way to work as an instructional designer. One way is not more pure than another. And third, instructional designers should consider the best fit for a combination of skills and other factors related to job satisfaction.

Someone may be happier working alone in a small organization than working in a team in a larger setting.

Designers and Failure

In everyone's work life, there are bad days when he or she makes mistakes. Designers are no different. If someone tried to write down every mistake he or she has made as a designer, it would challenge this book in length. Although it may seem unnecessary to mention this in an otherwise upbeat book, it warrants discussion.

Police cadets are often taught that the most dangerous times for police officers are the first six months and the last six months. New officers don't have the experience to always know what to do, and experienced officers have survived a long time and think nothing new can happen to them. Similarly, new designers have a higher probability of making mistakes because they lack experience. When they have been a designer for a while, they tend to get complacent and careless.

Recently an experienced designer was participating in several focus groups with high school students that their teachers attended as observers. This group was a little different from the usual population of adults the designer worked with. Not remembering that teachers like to teach, the designer sat in horror as a teacher got up and taught the students a lesson on the topic during the focus group.

That was a bad day for that veteran designer, but the designer did leave with some very important lessons:

- Make sure you have a plan and that everyone is clear on the process.
- Always follow the plan.

Sounds simple, but focus groups can get out of control and it takes a good facilitator to make them work the way they should. When those bad days come, it is good to remember that everyone goofs or gets complacent now and then.

Thinking Big

One tool that a designer needs to perfect is the practice of universality. To a designer that means designing as if his or her curriculum is going to be implemented in a thousand places at once by a thousand different facilitators. Another aspect of this concept is the notion that the designer will never see, meet, or come in contact with anyone that takes a course he or she has designed. This tool is important even if a designer plans to implement the course with a group of participants with whom he or she is familiar. It enables great designers to look outside their safety zone and review every aspect of a project as if the safety net of familiarity were removed.

This second aspect gets us to a very important issue with designers: separating design work from facilitating. Although some designers do actually play both the designer and facilitator roles, they should design the curriculum as if they will never play both roles.

A friend once commented to me that one of the more serious issues in the training environment was the great teacher complex. This malady usually affects facilitators who think they can just stand in front of a group of learners and impart wisdom by the barrelful.

Designers need to be cognizant of the great teacher traits in all of us. This malady will keep designers from preparing the kind of design that any facilitator can use. Instead, they will prepare a design for their own use on the assumption that they can handle any situation that might occur while they are facilitating a course. These designers may not consider a wide array of problems as they prepare their plans, including learners who ask questions far afield of the topic, whether the lesson will run short or long, and whether there is too much or too little content at an inappropriate level for the population.

Their disregard for these fundamental concerns is fine if no one else will ever use the designs, but that is not always the case. In fact, many designers never actually facilitate their designs.

A great tool for a designer's repertoire is the ability to wear only one hat at a time: designer or facilitator. Never try to wear both together. Confusion can occur when designers tend to rely on their facilitation skills and subject matter knowledge, instead of the analysis data, as this example shows. An instructional designer with a computer science background has the responsibility to design and facilitate a course for a common software package. The analysis shows that the facilitators are from within the organization and are good at using computers but have no background in computer science. For the course, the basis of the training is the designer's subject matter and facilitation skills. Although the designer includes key concepts in the lesson plan, there is very little detailed information about the workings of the program. The designer would have been able to provide that information in class, but the facilitators cannot fill in the blanks missing in the lesson plan. The course flops because the facilitators cannot provide the missing information, and the designer who has the knowledge is not the facilitator.

Every designer should use personal facilitator skills as one component of good design practice, but avoid the trap of leaving out key information or instructions based on one's personal ability to facilitate a particular course. It is a much better practice to put too much detail into a course instead of too little. Facilitators can always pick and choose from what is offered them.

The Value-Neutral Designer

Most of us have opinions. These opinions are based on any number of experiences, cultural and environmental influences, and the magazines that greet us in the checkout line at the grocery. It is natural to assume that these biases will travel with us as we conduct ourselves as designers. (Note that the skill of value-neutral designer differs from that of designer neutrality because this type of neutrality is based on values, not office politics.)

In the description of focus groups in chapter 2, it is asserted that neutrality is an important part of facilitating or designing these types of analysis vehicles. The same must be true of the entire process of designing curricula. If a designer wanders at all from the center of the road, focus might be lost.

The designer's tool of neutrality is not a natural instinct for most of us. Most of us must exercise a great deal of conscious effort to keep our opinions to ourselves. Some designers may argue that opinions are the very instrument that drove them to be a designer in the first place. It is important to remember that motivation based on content must be stripped from the process of instructional design.

Designers work in every conceivable type of environment from the desert heat of Egypt to the top floor of a multinational corporation. Neutrality relates to process and content, and in no way negates loyalty to the organization. A designer should stay out of the opinion business except in regard to design issues.

The following example will show what happens when neutrality is negated in the design process. An organization has requested a course on a controversial subject, perhaps sexual misconduct in the workplace. The topic attracts polarized opinions and has tainted the workplace culture. As the designer visits the cafeteria for refills of hours-old coffee, employees ask about the design department's views of the subject. Should the designer express an opinion, the credibility of the design work would be eliminated. The designer's efforts would be negated, no matter what opinion the designer expresses.

Putting What You Have Learned Into Action

The exercises that follow will give you a chance to fine-tune your skills.

Exercise 10.1. Mental strategies.

These are some important questions a designer should ask in order to start developing and nurturing that sixth sense that great designers seem to acquire:

- Have I determined if the need is instructional or noninstructional?
- Have I asked the client what success means for him or her in this project?
- Do I have a handle on all of the constraints and resources for this project?
- Is there something I can do to challenge me as a designer?

Now it is your turn. What strategies are important for you to adopt in your designer roles?

1. _____
   _____

2. _____
   _____

3. _____
   _____

4. _____
   _____

5. _____
   _____

Exercise 10.2. Role conflict.

Name several strategies designers can take to minimize the risk of role conflict during a project. The example is to get you started.

1. Agree on project tasks before beginning.

2. _____

3. _____

4. _____

5. _____

Exercise 10.3. Jargon control.

List several jargon words from this book and think of ways that each term could have been explained in a better way. The example is to get you started.

1. SME—should be referred to as subject matter experts or perhaps content experts.

2. _____

3. _____

4. _____

5. _____

Exercise 10.4. Designer neutrality.

List several situations (perhaps from your experience) that required neutrality. The example is to get you started.

1. Never express an opinion about controversial subjects unrelated to instructional design or my role in a project, such as comments about someone's promotion.

2. _____
   _____

3. _____
   _____

4. _____
   _____

5. _____
   _____

Exercise 10.5. Types of designers.

List several different roles you might like to play as a designer and explain why each seems attractive to you. The example is to get you started.

1. Design a project by myself for someone else to implement. This removes the safety net of being familiar with the learners and allows real growth as a designer.

2. _____
   _____

3. _____
   _____

4. _____
   _____

5. _____
   _____

Exercise 10.6. Designers and failure.

List several examples from your past that moved you from possible failure to success. Chart the growth you experienced as a result of the process. The example is to get you started.

1. Missing a deadline forced me to mentally reinvest in the project and do a better job of getting the project completed on time.

2. _____
   _____

3. _____
   _____

4. _____
   _____

5. _____
   _____

Exercise 10.7. Thinking big.

List several examples of ways in which a designer could make a course universally acceptable to different levels of facilitators. The example is to get you started.

1. Provide detailed information on the content for facilitators who may lack certain background knowledge.

2. _____
   _____

3. _____
   _____

4. _____
   _____

5. _____
   _____

Exercise 10.8. Value neutral design.

List several situations that require a designer to be neutral. The example is to get you started.

1. Facilitating differences of opinion about course content.

2. _____
   _____

3. _____
   _____

4. _____
   _____

5. _____
   _____

11

Designing for Web-Based Training

Zane L. Berge and Marie de Verneil

Today's global economy causes the workplace to face significant, continuous demand for learning new skills and knowledge and at an increasingly fast pace. Organizations are using the Web to deliver instruction and provide content because it is easily accessible (Ethernet card or modem) and flexible (almost instant editing) and can naturally provide a very rich learning environment.

Although not all online training and education is Web based, the trend in the workplace is clearly toward the Web and Web tools. In this chapter, the terms **online** and **Web based** are used synonymously. The term **online training** means computer-mediated training as opposed to such things as video-conferencing. Designing Web-based instruction (WBI) is not a whole lot more complex than designing any other technology-based learning. However, it does call for a process in which concurrent and dynamic elements must meet to create a successful hypermedia learning environment. The capabilities of the Web are expansive, and, therefore, so are the elements to coordinate and manage in designing instruction.

This chapter provides guidelines for designers, developers, and instructors in the workplace as they make the transition from face-to-face classroom instruction to Web-based instruction (Berge and Dougherty, 1999). The framework involves four dynamic and interrelated perspectives: managerial, instructional, technical, and social (Berge, 1995). This chapter focuses on the managerial and instructional issues in the development of Web-based training, with a lesser emphasis on the technical and social aspects. Even so, all four areas are interrelated and overlapping in many cases because it is often impossible to categorize an issue in a single area, even though it is done so here for convenience.

Managerial Considerations

Managerial considerations, also described by some authors as procedural or administrative, include among other things, conducting the fiscal and political environmental scans in which training takes place, the strategic planning aspects, and support services.

Organizational Needs

It cannot be emphasized too greatly that the biggest factor in the long-term success of a training program is that it meets a business need. It is necessary to determine how an organization views distance training. Only if a designer is meeting a need of the organization will resource allocation and organizational change take place with regard to the activities under development. Creating online courses is often a time-consuming, labor-intensive process, and the developer must be careful to determine what to expect from other persons in the organization, such as how much time subject matter experts will have available for the project under consideration.

Trainees' Needs

Some of the reasons training managers have moved toward anyplace, anytime delivery of training are that it saves money in travel expenses and keeps trainees on the job, not in the training room for days or weeks at a time. But are the learners ready for this? An audience analysis can often uncover some barriers that have the potential to cause online learning to be ineffective. It is often assumed that the audience consists of adult learners for whom asynchronicity (time and space independence) is crucial. Although that may be so, there needs to be attention given to such things as how convenient the participants' access is to the Web, how experienced they are with online learning and computer use overall, and whether they like this mode of deliver or not. This form of training delivery most often uses a good amount of asynchronous (that is, not real time) learning. That characteristic is useful in overcoming some of the potential problems, but it also relies on much more self-motivation from each of the participants. The implications of unmotivated participants in a self-paced system are obvious—effective training that is hit or miss.

Program Support

The support the program receives in the organization should match the organization's needs. An organization should plan and budget support, such as technical assistance, time from subject matter experts, instructional and graphic design, computer programming and authoring, and basic office operations.

Some of the managerial tasks include:

- identifying stakeholders to analyze existing and potential support.
- identifying distance learning programs and events already taking place within the organization. Interviewing involved instructors, designers, and managers about technical help and other infrastructure that may be available to share.
- identifying instructors who are currently using WBI, and the instructor training that is available to see if there are marginal resources available for future programs. (Although instructors using WBI are not expected to become technical wizards, they should be aware of software and hardware capabilities that constitute the environment in which teaching and learning will take place.)
- participating in existing distance learning professional groups. Meeting other people who are active and responsible for online training inside and outside your organization often causes a collaborative environment to WBI development that is critical to success.

Instructional Considerations

Define the Learning

The same questions surrounding good instructional design need to be asked and answered regardless of delivery systems. Is the learning you are designing ill defined, which would call for a different design than a sequential, procedural part in a program? Is it well suited for bringing together multiple perspectives on a variety of themes? Should a designer try to duplicate a face-to-face environment, or should the designer take advantage of the Web's hypermedia environment to develop new learning strategies? The traditional lecture could be replaced by a short presentation (text based or audiovideo streamed so that learners can hear and view the media over the Internet without first having to wait for it to download), which will contextualize thematically organized Websites listed for the participants. A conferencing system can allow discussion among learners and instructors or collectively resolve the problems outlined in the program.

Traditional Versus Nontraditional Instruction

In a discussion of WBI, it would be easy to equate a new delivery medium (the Web) with "a new pedagogy" and, consequently, define face-to-face, in-person, classroom training as being a traditional, old, "bad" approach to instruction. This is misleading. It is not the delivery medium that defines the instruction. Granted, the delivery medium is instrumental in the learning approach, and its capabilities should be integrated in the instructional design. When an instructional event such as a lecture, for instance, is replaced by a talking head on streamed video, the delivery mode is more high tech, but the instructional strategy has not changed.

The nature of the learning should determine the design of the learning environment. There are different types of interaction: between learner and instructor, between learner and content, and among learners (Berge, 1999). Included in the online learning environment are synchronous (real-time) and asynchronous conferencing, assessment tools, and class management tools. Technically, almost any element or strategy that designers, facilitators, or learners can use in person, they can also use online. Effectiveness is really a matter of the instructional design, not the system used to deliver it.

Bourne, McMaster, Rieger, and Campbell (1997) have analyzed how well the common instructional methods fare in an online, asynchronous learning system. Learning by listening (that is, lectures) can be implemented by on-screen video played on demand or downloaded. Its likely success is fair to poor. This model suffers because the lecturer is not present, but one of its benefits is that it permits replaying and indexing the content. Discovery learning, such as library and literature searches, can be conducted on the Web and often yields much better results than traditional library searches. However, there is a lot of garbage online, and novice trainees-as-researchers may not know how to separate the wheat from the chaff. Online methods like learning modules, simulations, and electronic writing and critiquing are methods by which people can learn by doing, as they would in laboratories and in other forms of writing and creating things. Online systems are an excellent media for writing and critiquing, but online laboratory materials are not widespread. Finally, learning through discussion and debates does not fare well with large numbers of learners all at once, but can be excellent in small classes with the right instructor.

Designing Web-Based Instruction

There are dozens of models and approaches to teaching and learning. But essentially, there are two major frameworks from which to view training and education. In the first, content and knowledge determined by someone else is transmitted to the learner via lecture, textbook, videotape, or some other way. In the second, a learner transforms information, generates hypotheses, and makes decisions about the knowledge he or she is constructing, or socially constructing through communication with others (Berge, 1998; McManus, 1996).

The framework in which content is transmitted to another person, presumably more novice at that particular set of knowledge or skills, is often called an **objectivist approach.** The objectivist models most often describe interaction between the teacher and the learner and between the learner and the content, but there is little consideration given to peer interaction. The alternative framework described above is a **constructivist approach.** Constructivists view the mind as a processor, rather than a container. New ideas are internalized or processed according to that which is already existing or is known within the individual's thinking. Al Mekhlafi (1997) describes constructivism as follows:

> Constructivists believe that our personal world is constructed in our minds and that these personal constructions define our personal realities. According to this belief, the mind is the instrument of thinking which interprets events, objects, and perspectives rather than seeking to remember and comprehend an objective knowledge. Constructivists engage the learners so that the knowledge they construct is not inert, but rather usable in new and different situations. Constructivist environments engage learners in knowledge construction through collaborative activities that embed learning in a meaningful context and through reflection on what has been learned through conversations with other learners. (Mekhlafi, 1997, p.1).

It is easy to see how the Web environment would be an ideal learning platform for people who hold this frame of mind. It brings together in an authentic setting, multiple global perspectives on very diverse subjects and provides professional expertise that learners can use to develop their own learning structures. However, access to information is but one part of the equation. As with any learning, the learner must engage with the environment in meaningful ways.

Designing for Transfer

The objectivists most often describe learning outcomes in terms of exhibited behaviors. As a result of an instructional analysis, designers set the performance objectives. Ritchie and Hoffman (1997) have proposed an objectivist WBI implementation model based on the following seven instructional sequences:

- **Motivating the learner:** Designers motivate learners through external stimuli, such as a multimedia Webpage with graphics, sound, or animation, and an inquiry, such as an interesting problem or mystery to be solved. However it is done, the designers' key to motivation is to establish the relevance of what is to be learned to the perceived needs of the learner.

- **Identifying what is to be learned:** Usually, designers explicitly list the outcomes or expectations, which trainees access on an instructional page. Additionally, designers can help learners focus on the task at hand with such techniques as limiting external links to what is of critical importance to the learning objectives.

- **Reminding learners of past knowledge:** On the basis of the learners' profiles, designers can provide links that will help the learners contextualize the new knowledge to be learned.

- **Requiring active involvement by requiring the learners to do a project.** A project might be, for example, to explore the principles of accounting by producing a profit-and-loss statement for the learner's own business.

- **Providing guidance and feedback during exploration of Web materials:** Designers can assist learners by labeling links with such descriptive terms as **example** or **shortest path.** Additionally, the designer can often provide guidance and feedback by requiring learners to make a choice among alternatives and provide feedback pages with the answers.

- **Testing:** As organizations evolve and mature in the use of WBI, they may create templates and other tools to make the technical development of online evaluation easier. Similarly, as organizations mature, they may offer Web-editing tools to participants so that they can more easily create an end product for their projects that is suitable for evaluation by the instructor and peers.

- **Providing enrichment and remediation:** The Web is rich with content and resources. It may be appropriate for designers to link pages in a systematic or organized way for learners to enrich their learning. Depending on the type of learners taking the program, costs, and other management considerations, designers may wish to provide alternative methods of information, presentation, and ways to master the instructional objectives.

Designing for a Constructivist's Approach

Constructivists have proposed various theories and principles relating to teaching and learning, but one of the most appropriate for a Web-based environment is cognitive flexibility theory (CFT) (Jonassen and others, 1997). Essentially, researchers developed CFT to overcome oversimplification and the use of prearranged knowledge that they believed did not prepare learners to face real-life complexity. Adherents of CFT believe in presenting content from multiple and often irreconcilable perspectives. Web-based instruction designed from CFT strives to be authentic above almost everything else. It presents varied cases from multiple points of view to provide learners with a variety of applied contexts from which they will construct personal knowledge (Berge, 1997). McManus (1996) has proposed a CFT instructional model composed of seven elements:

1. **Define the learning domain:** In an ill-structured environment, designers need to set the boundaries around what is to be learned.

2. **Identify cases within the domain:** Designers need to identify the various elements or cases to be studied: the bits of declarative and procedural knowledge, text, graphics, sounds, and videos that represent the domain.

3. **Identify themes and perspectives (guided path):** In this model, designers often present the learner with two alternatives: the guided path or the learner-controlled path (the next description). The guided path will identify designers' goals and select learning elements that they believe are important. These goals and elements differ from traditional ISD learning objectives in that they are suggestions and not what the learner will necessarily get out of the environment.

4. **Learner-controlled path:** The learner-controlled path allows the learner to decide what is important to learn within the defined learning domains. If learners create their own objectives, they need to be provided with the tools they will need to explore the learning domain on their own. For example, some tools are keyword search engines and concept maps that can be restructured by the learner.

5 and 6. **Map multiple paths through cases to show themes and perspectives:** Designers create links between the instructional elements that represent the cases for their suggested path or paths. These should reflect multiple perspectives.

7. **Encourage learner self-reflection:** Although typically there is no standard objective evaluation, designers can provide questions or guidance to promote the learner's self-evaluation, including suggestions on what to do next.

Social Aspect of Web-Based Instruction

Often, both objectivists and constructivists have one thing in common: They do not address the learning as a social process. Although most models do not exclude the possibility of peer learning, it is important in most Web-based instruction that a designer explicitly include learning in a social context. Often learning can be seen as a process of exchanging ideas, thoughts, and feelings among people. The result is often a new way of viewing the world or new ways of behaving (Lauzon, 1992). In this framework, discussion is a key learning strategy. However, the social dimension may go further. Lave and Wenger state that:

> ... the key factors in supporting learning are those which makes a community open to its newcomers, allowing them to participate in its practices and move from peripheral to central status as rapidly and smoothly as possible. (Lave and Wenger, 1991, in Wegerif, 1998, p. 2).

In WBI, these factors should translate into a design that will deliberately focus on developing a virtual community in which all members will feel centrally participating. This community can be achieved, but it takes work on the parts of the learners and the instructor. Facilitators can help create this community by taking steps like the following:

- Ask participants to post a biography (with picture if possible).
- Require active participation from all participants. Instructors should privately contact learners who are not participating and use moderating skills to encourage their involvement. These skills include identifying technical or other barriers that keep them from participating and helping to overcome them. Especially in the beginning, instructors or facilitators need to acknowledge and show appreciation for participants' contributions (Berge, 1995).
- Provide a virtual café designated for socializing purposes.
- Offer chat rooms in the Web-based environment for participants who want an area for real-time, social interaction.

Technical Aspects of Web-Based Instruction

General Guidelines

The instructor or facilitator of Web-based training must attend to certain technical matters that usually do not surface with in-person classrooms. Some of these listed below are general in nature, whereas others have more specifically to do with the learning environment or the homepage design and use.

- Facilitators must secure ongoing technical assistance from information technology (IT) or from a stable internal or external source for such assistance. Usually, the IT staff will help set up the course site (that is, introduce Web-based instructional package) and password privileges and create other set-up features. Ongoing support is critical to the success of training programs, and most organizations assign one or more technical liaisons on a full-time or part-time basis to support operations. As a rule, learners' computer systems must meet a minimal hardware and software configuration to help streamline support functions.

- Instructors should provide online tutoring if they are using a sophisticated Web-based instructional package.

- Depending on the program's overall timeline, instructors should allow adequate time after the start of the training to work out bugs, especially in new systems, and problems participants may have.

- Instructors should provide enrolled participants with instructions (perhaps mailed if they are new to WBI) and with a variety of ways of contacting the instructor, such as by email, phone, and fax.

- Instructors who use summative evaluations should consider privacy issues when they decide whether or not to mail them.

Understanding the Nature of the Environment

A strength of Web learning is that it is a nonlinear method of organizing and displaying multimedia information (text, graphics, sound, and video). Eklund (1996) proposes that designers use the following guidelines to maximize learning using WBI:

- Use a subject matter expert's knowledge of the domain to form a concept map of the subject matter and to base the links within the WBI environment.

- Incorporate advanced navigational devices (such as maps) to inform the users of where they are and where they have been (for example, fading or changing the color of visited links).

- Provide adaptive advice, based on several typical users, and model the learner's acquisition of knowledge. Consider suggesting a preferred path through the knowledge base if one exists.

Proper Labels

To take advantage of the Web-based environment, the homepage and Website should direct participants to alternative paths that reflect the different stages of understanding. Learners choose different nonlinear paths through the instructional materials according to their own level of expertise in the subject matter and knowledge of hypermedia environments (Eklund, 1996). Following are some possible labels:

- Labels such as **Tell me more, more examples like this one,** and **what do the experts say** will help learners choose the path that fits them best.

- Different tools can help learners in different ways. Navigational tools can help users move to another location, structural tools can provide an overview map and indexes, and historical tools can help learners see where they have been.

- It is helpful to stay within existing Web standards as much as possible so that experienced Web users will recognize and be able to navigate as they are used to doing on the Web.

The Homepage

There are advantages to designing a homepage for the program that is on the company intranet even if the course is contained in a Web-based conferencing software program such as FirstClass Intranet Server, Lotus Domino, Oracle InterOffice, WebBoard, or WebCT. The company's intranet could serve as a point from which learners can access the proprietary software. (For a comprehensive guide to software that powers discussions on the Web, designers should see David R. Woolley's, **Conferencing Software for the Web** at http://thinkofit.com/webconf/#commercial.)

- **Instructional considerations:**
  - The homepage could be an advance organizer, providing participants with important links and access to major databases. The Webpage should give participants a feel of the learning environment and engage them in further exploration.

  - There should be a course description even if designers intend posting this information on their Web conferencing software, which often cannot be accessed by visitors.

  - The syllabus and a course management description should be on the homepage. Designers should keep in mind intellectual property rights issues (that is, What are they willing to divulge to casual visitors to the Webpage?).

  - They should provide an email address to send inquiries.

- **Graphic considerations**
  - Speed is a key factor with graphics or animated graphics interchange formats, known as **gifs.** Computer users want pictures that download quickly so it is best to avoid big pictures and to slice pictures for faster downloading, especially if modems are involved in the users' systems.
  - Patterned backgrounds are hard to read and distract from content.
  - Some colors are hard to read (such as many pastels), and some complementary colors clash (like red with black).
  - Designers should check how their work will look on different platforms. Colors do not always transfer properly from one operating system to another.
  - Designers should check how different browsers will handle their pages.
  - It is best to design for the middle ground (speed of the modem and browser).
  - Designers should provide text versions of their images when possible and appropriate (that is, when the instructional goals are not compromised by so doing).
  - Designers should consider how the screen image will look printed. Some colors will not show well on a printer. Try to print before uploading to the server.

- **Course material considerations:**
  - Course participants should get all assigned reading material online with the exception of any assigned textbooks. Some of the materials may already be available online. Designers should arrange to put others there. Copyright issues apply because the protection of intellectual property is a legal issue that designers should not overlook. Working out the copyright and any intellectual property agreements can be a lengthy process and should be discussed early in the development process.

- **Troubleshooting:**
  - There should be online help, even if simply an email address for problems and a frequently asked questions (FAQ) list.
  - There could be a special Trouble Shooting Forum within the course conferencing system or course management system at

which all could share insights and technical problems could be addressed and indexed.

— Dead URLs (that is, those no longer in use) should also be identified as soon as possible and deleted.

— Instructors should request feedback for all major activities. Learners should provide written comments (such as that there are too many readings) and be engaged in the design process. Instructors should be flexible and react positively to this feedback.

- **Evaluations:**

  — **Formative evaluation:** Subject matter, teaching style, and the educational philosophy (objectivist versus constructivist) will dictate the course subject matter assessment. Designers can use traditional assessment instruments such as quizzes (multiple choice and so on), which are available in most Web-based instructional software, or use CGI or Java scripts to develop their own.

  — **Summative evaluation:** Although designers can **plan** for a summative evaluation that aligns with the content, objectives, and goals for the course, and the practice and activities in which the learners engage, instructors and stakeholders do not often use a summative evaluation of the course to report to appropriate stakeholders and decision makers. It is usually difficult to gather the data needed to link instruction and training to job performance.

Conclusion

Developing online courses is a team-based, synergetic process that must address managerial, instructional, social, and technical considerations. Although managerial and technical considerations do provide the necessary infrastructure for the online course, they are subordinate to instructional considerations. The designer must also account for the fact that learning takes place in a social context and create a Web-based environment that may maximize learning.

References

Berge, Z.L. (1995). "Facilitating Computer Conferencing: Recommendations From the Field." *Educational Technology, 35*(1), 22–30.

Berge, Z.L. (1997). "Characteristics of Online Teaching in Post-Secondary, Formal Education." *Educational Technology, 37*(3), 35–47.

Berge, Z.L. (1998). "Conceptual Frameworks in Distance Training and Education." In *Distance Training: How Innovative Organizations Are Using Technology to Maximize Learning and Meet Business Objectives*, D.A. Schreiber and Z.L. Berge, editors. San Francisco: Jossey-Bass, 19–36.

Berge, Z.L. (1999). "Interaction in Post-Secondary, Web-Based Learning and Teaching." *Educational Technology, 29*(1), 5–11.

Berge, Z.L., and K. Dougherty. (1999). "How to Convert Face-to-Face Instruction to Web-Based Instruction." In *Training and Performance Sourcebook*, Mel Siberman, editor. New York: McGraw-Hill, 323–330.

Bourne, J.R., E. McMaster, J. Rieger, and J.O. Campbell. (1997). "Paradigms for On-line Learning." *JALN, 1*(2), [Online at http://www.aln.org/alnweb/journal/jaln_Vol1issue2.htm.]

Eklund, J. (1996). "Cognitive Models for Structuring Hypermedia and Implications for Learning from the World-Wide Web. [Online at http://www.scu.edu.au/sponsored/ausweb95/papers/hypertext/eklund/index.html.]

Jonassen, D.H., D. Dyer, K. Peters, T. Robinson, D. Harvey, M. King, and P. Loughner. (1997). *Cognitive Flexibility Hypertexts on the Web*. In *Web-Based Instruction*, B.H. Khan, editor. Englewood Cliffs, NJ: Educational Technology Publications.

Lauzon, A.C. (1992). "Integrating Computer-Based Instruction With Computer Conferencing: An Evaluation of a Model for Designing Online Education." *The American Journal of Distance Education, 6*(2), 32–46.

McManus, T.F. (1996). *Delivering Instruction on the World-Wide Web*. [Online at http://ccwf.cc.utexas.edu/%7Emcmanus/WBI.html.]

Mekhlafi, A. (1997). *Constructivism*. [Online at http://seamonkey.ed.asu.edu/~mcisaac/emc703old97/spring97/7/mekh7.htm.]

Ritchie, D.C., and B. Hoffman. (1997). "Incorporating Instructional Design Principles With the World Wide Web." In *Web-Based Instruction*, B.H. Khan, editor. Englewood Cliffs, NJ: Educational Technology Publications.

Wegerif, R. (1998). "The Social Dimension of Asynchronous Learning Networks." *JALN, 2*(1). [Online at http://www.aln.org.alnweb/journal/vol2_issue1/wegerif.htm.]

The Authors

Zane L. Berge is director of training systems in the Instructional Systems Development Graduate Program at the University of Maryland Baltimore County. Prior to this, he directed and founded the Center for Teaching and Technology at Georgetown University in Washington, D.C. His work in computer-mediated communication in education includes his notable series of books: a three-volume set, *Computer-Mediated Communication and the Online Classroom*, published in 1995, which encompasses higher and distance education; and a four-volume set, *Wired Together: Computer-Mediated Communication in the K-12 Classroom*, published in 1997. In 1998, he co-edited with D.A. Schreiber the award-winning book *Distance Training: How*

Innovative Organizations Are Using Technology to Maximize Learning and Meet Business Objectives. His latest book, *Sustaining Distance Training*, is in press. Berge has a Ph.D. from Michigan State University in educational systems development. He may be contacted at berge@umbc.edu.

Marie de Verneil holds an M.A. and a Ph.D. from the Catholic University of America and an M.A. in instructional design from the University of Maryland Baltimore County (UMBC). For the past 12 years, she had been the editor-in-chief and senior writer of France-TV Magazine, a French news video magazine distributed in the United States by PBS. For the program, she developed a new video methodology for foreign language acquisition. She is presently the director of the France-TV Magazine project and is designing an online certificate for French for business. She is the coordinator, trainer, and supervisor of all the French lower-level courses at UMBC. Her current interest focuses on the use of computer-mediated communication in the foreign language classroom. Marie de Verneil has co-authored a first-year French textbook *Objectif France*, published in 1993 by Heinle & Heinle, and she has published and presented various articles on video-based foreign language learning. Her present research is on Web-based instruction and how to integrate a constructivist and communicative approach in a distance learning setting.

12

Wrapping it Up

There isn't a single, individual element of instructional design that is all that difficult to learn or to use. As with any other professional pursuit, mastering a basic set of skills and learning the tricks of the trade bring it all together. The process of designing training may appear easy to people outside the process. After all, well-designed training does appear seamless as it is being implemented. That is one of the ironies of design: The better the course goes, the less chance there is that anyone will appreciate the effort that went into it.

Designers who use the design and lesson plan approach presented here have the opportunity to combine a number of instructional design skills and, as a result, to construct almost any training project that makes its way to their door.

Most designers incorporate elements of a design plan or a lesson plan in their work. However, they may never have known what each separate element is called or even its full value. For example, a designer may have incorporated a course rationale into a verbal presentation to a client without understanding why it made a difference to the course, or a designer may have written facilitator prerequisites without studying why they matter in the project. In the case of lesson plans, many designers use some type of format but may have never realized that there was a sequence that supports the way a participant learns and retains information. Without a complete understanding of the elements of the design and lesson plans, designers may not take the necessary steps consistently and may not follow through with them in a way that will benefit the learners.

Designers' jobs are easier when they see ISD as a process and have names for the different elements. Their good instincts about how best to design a project then combine with a system's approach to training and education to provide a solid foundation for design.

Following is an overview of this book's systems approach to developing training. ISD is represented by a number of well-thought-out models, but designers most commonly use the ADDIE model. ADDIE stands for analysis, design, development, implementation, and evaluation. Designers should work toward developing their own ISD model based on their experience and support systems like this book. Most designers end up doing that anyway, although most are unaware of what they have created.

The ADDIE Model

A summary of each of the five elements in the ADDIE model of ISD follows:

Analysis

During the analysis phase of ISD, a designer needs to make sure that every atom of data is collected. Designers need to be data magnets and attract everything of value into the design process. They must:

- Ask every question and not move on without an answer.
- Fill boxes full of results from Web searches or other data if necessary.
- Conduct focus groups or undertake other data-gathering methods as necessary.

When they have gathered all the data, designers need to ask four questions:

1. How will learners be different after the training? Will they have a new skill, knowledge, or ability, such as enhanced language capabilities or a better way to process anger in the workplace? Designers should always determine the objectives.

2. How will learners meet the objectives? Have the distribution and instructional methods been selected? The choices are endless, but designers must decide methods early in the process to eliminate wasted time and energy later.

3. How will designers know when the learners have met the objectives? Have designers decided which of the evaluation methods are appropriate for their objectives and methods? Designers should prepare evaluations at the same time that they write the objectives.

4. How does the sponsor of the training define success? If the sponsor's expectations are unknown, there is little chance of ever making him or her happy. It is almost impossible to hit a moving target. Designers have to ask until they get an answer.

Design

Design is the unique element of ISD, with no professional equivalent in other fields. It is here that the project gets a designer's touch. Designers prepare the objectives and evaluation tasks, writing, rewriting, and writing again until they work. They choose the distribution and instructional methods, and prepare drafts of materials and media. During design, the data gathered in analysis evolves into the clarity and purpose that a project needs to be successful. A design plan becomes the blueprint for the rest of a project.

Development

Development is pasting the project together. Sometimes designers do it all and develop their own materials and media. Other times they are responsible for managing the process. It can be challenging to work with computer programmers, graphic artists, compositors, video producers, and printers, but it is also satisfying to see ideas become great materials, ready for final production after pilot testing.

Pilot testing ensures that a project is ready for the big time before it moves to implementation. Actors rehearse their lines before a play opens, and musicians practice for hours to perfect a melody before an audience hears a note. In similar fashion, designers use pilot tests to give training an opportunity to muff its lines or hit a wrong note before learners have an opportunity to take a course.

Designers shouldn't get discouraged if they end up doing the design and development work without any help. Multimedia CDs, four-color manuals, and videos with high production values are the exception to the rule for training design. Most organizations can't afford to implement every project on the Web or have materials that have the appearance of a coffee table book. The resources and funding for design work are still largely limited.

Implementation

Implementation usually finds designers in front of the learners or in back of them. Designers may be facilitating, evaluating, or both. Until people outside of the process of ISD acquire an appreciation of all the work that goes into it, they are not likely to be aware of any ISD element but implementation. However, designers know that implementation is the ISD equivalent of hanging a newly completed painting. The work is now ready for appreciation.

Designers make sure that the evaluation plan is in effect and that all of the information from the evaluation process is gathered. The facilitator may make necessary changes in the training on the fly during implementation, or the designer will make them later, as the dust settles.

Evaluation

Evaluation, the fifth element in the ADDIE model, is always looking over a designer's shoulders. Just as three-year-old children believe that Santa knows if they have been good or bad, evaluation always knows whether training has met the mark. Santa and evaluation share the same quality of vigilance. The difference between good training and bad training is listening to what evaluation has to say. This is very hard to do if a designer does not allow evaluation to be a major component of the design process.

Kirkpatrick (1998) has given designers a brilliant framework for evaluation: four different boxes in which most evaluation needs fit. A designer may want to use two, three, or all of these levels of evaluation, depending on the needs.

Level one evaluations are based on learners' reactions to training. Did they like it? Did they find it worth their investment of time? Did the distribution and instructional methods find favor with the learners? Were the bagels fresh and the coffee hot? These are all reactions to the training, every single moment of it.

Level two evaluations are the same as the evaluations written for objectives. Designers are measuring each learner's ability to meet an objective. Designers must always be sure that the learner is meeting objectives.

Level three evaluations are the way to determine if the training made any difference in a learner's ability to meet the objectives. It is not unusual for evaluations to be performed three, six, or even 12 months after the training. This information allows a designer to compare results and determine the staying power of the training.

Level four evaluations measure the return-on-investment (ROI) of a project. While usually best left to the accountants because of the financial nature of the process, ROI has a place in most projects and designers should not ignore the long-term value that they bring. Large corporations can calculate ROI in the millions of dollars; a community group can figure ROI by the number of new adult readers who can perform a valuable skill. Either way, designers' work has value, and they should think about the impact the training may have on the learner or sponsor.

Accumulation of Advantages

The introduction to this book mentioned the term **accumulation of advantages.** It is the process of performing a number of separate design skills that meld together to become a finished design project. All of the ADDIE elements need to be present for an accumulation of advantages to exist. Doing less than five phases, such as eliminating analysis and evaluation, offers little hope for a successful training project. Accumulate all of the advantages offered by utilizing ISD and reaping the benefits of well-conceived and delivered training.

Rechecking Your Skills

Now that you have completed all of the chapters, you can evaluate how your ending skills compare with those when you began this book. This is a pre- and postevaluation of your progress. Look through the list in table 9 and answer the questions "yes" or "no." When you are done, compare your answers to the Skills Inventory you completed in the Introduction. How did you do? If you are still uncertain about any of these instructional design elements, review the chapter associated with the skill.

Table 9. Skills inventory.

Do You Know How to:	Yes	No
Conduct a population analysis		
Design and implement a focus group session		
Write four-part objectives		
Name the four objective domains		
Define and provide examples of at least three instructional methods		
Define and provide examples of at least three distribution methods		
Write at least two evaluation tasks		
Explain the performance agreement principle using an example		
Design evaluations for each of the four Kirkpatrick levels		
Complete a design plan		
Construct a lesson plan		

The Power of ISD

The real power of ISD lies in its ability to provide a foundation for the instructional design process. The work that builds from this foundation can have numerous variations to fit designers' changing needs. The system itself is endlessly evolving within the mind and imagination of each separate designer. This process is only as rigid as a designer wants it to be.

Readers are free to play a dominant role in its evolution by revising the ideas in this book to fit their particular needs. With the new skills now in their inventories, they are ready to meet any challenge.

Reference

Kirkpatrick, Donald. (1998). *Evaluating Training Programs: The Four Levels* (2d edition). San Francisco: Berrett-Koehler.

Appendix

Lesson Plan

Following is a complete lesson plan for Poison Prevention in the Home. You may follow this model as you design a lesson plan for your course.

Implementation time: 1 hour

Materials: Home Poisoning video, flip charts and pens, sign-in sheets, evaluation forms, one set of handouts, one set of poison prevention brochures, blank paper for drawing maps and name tags. All materials for learners should be in lots of at least 10 percent more than the anticipated attendance.

Equipment: Laptop computer with the presentation software, computer projector and screen, extension cord, and surge protector.

Room arrangement: Classroom style with tables.

24-Hour Checklist

Day before: Confirm room assignment, confirm equipment list, test laptop and software, check computer projector, confirm all materials are ready.

One hour before the course starts: Confirm all room and equipment needs are met, test the equipment, test the computer and software, check the computer projector and connect to the computer, test the computer-projection link and readiness.

Now we need to actually begin the course. The instructions to the facilitator can take many forms. This lesson plan uses the nine events for our guide. The first event is gaining attention, for which we are going to show a short video. Following is how the lesson plan will look in our facilitator's guide:

To be completed before starting: Be sure the VCR is ready to be played. Check where the tape is cued and make sure it is at the right point so you can play it without further preparation. Unless you have a copy of the original video, the tape only contains the portion to be used here so that rewinding will get you within several seconds of the start.

Be sure the computer and computer projector are operating and that the software is operating.

Show frame #1, welcome to "Poison Prevention in the Home."

Prestart: Call the group together and start the course.

Introduce yourself and formally welcome the learners.

Noise Reduction—4 minutes

Advance to frame #2, poison threat.

In your own words . . .

Poisons are a constant threat in all of our homes. We have become so used to having poisons around us that we seldom pay any attention to their presence.

Advance to frame #3, video teaser.

In your own words . . .

As we watch this short video, see what happens to the Wilson family when they discover too late the dangers associated with poisons in the home.

Put computer projector on standby.

Show video (3 minutes).

In your own words . . .

As we work together to lessen the potential danger of poisons in your home, use the Wilson family's sad experience to serve as a warning to how quickly poisons can forever change your life.

Direction—3 minutes

Turn computer projector on.

Advance to frame #4, objectives.

In your own words . . .

We are going to be spending an hour together this evening and before you leave you should be able to:

- Identify different types of poisons in and around your home.
- Make a list of possible poison danger zones in your home.
- Prepare a map of your home highlighting all of the potential danger spots for poisons.
- Describe the first steps to take in the event of a possible poisoning.
- Contact the local Poison Center.

Recall—5 minutes

Advance to frame #5, poison statistics.
In your own words . . .

Poisons cause thousands of deaths every year in the United States. It is estimated that a vast majority of these deaths could be prevented.

Advance to frame #6, poison definition.
In your own words . . .

A poison is defined as any substance that can cause negative symptoms. Even a rash is considered to be a negative reaction when determining if something is a poison.

Advance to frame #7, poison labels and icons.
In your own words . . .

In this country poisons are required to be labeled to identify them as a dangerous substance. Several icons can designate a poison, and I am sure that you have seen many or all of these either in your home or at work.

As you prepare the poison hazard map for you home, you will need to identify which products actually present a potential hazard. You should never rely solely on labels and icons to identify poisons. It is not unusual for chemicals to be stored in unmarked containers after they have been moved from their original packaging. And, of course, the new container is very unlikely to be correctly labeled.

Advance to frame #8, brochure pages.
In your own words . . .

In your brochure, on pages 3 and 4, you will see drawings of a number of labels and icons used to represent poisons.

Content—15 minutes

Advance to frame #9, killers.

In your own words . . .

Your home is a deadly place to live. Under your counters and hiding in your closets are killers. Nestled away in your garage are veteran life threateners. These killers don't care at all about age, gender, or religion. In fact, they don't even care if you are a human or an animal. They are indiscriminate killers with no boundaries and no conscience.

Advance to frame #10, hiding places.

In your own words . . .

They are hiding in bottles, cans, and boxes. They are of various sizes and colors, and they all look so harmless as they lay in waiting for an unsuspecting victim. They seem so innocent until you have fallen into their trap and succumb to their danger.

Let's look at some of these villains and start exposing them to the public.

Advance to frame #11, types of poisons.

In your own words . . .

There are four general types of poisons that we are going to investigate tonight. They are household products, drugs, plants, and miscellaneous items.

Advance to frame #12, household products.

In your own words . . .

Household products include insecticides and vermin poisons, antifreeze, cleaning products, flea killers, and heavy metals like zinc and lead. Pets are especially endangered by fertilizers.

Advance to frame #13, drugs.

In your own words . . .

While all drugs should be considered poisonous, we need to remember that even products commonly left out such as acetaminophen, ibuprofen, and aspirin are dangerous to children and animals.

Drugs also present the largest risk of pet poisonings with nearly 75 percent of pet poisonings coming from drugs.

Advance to frame #14, plants.

In your own words . . .

> Plants are not usually considered poisoning risks, but they certainly pose lethal problems for animals. Several examples are Japanese yew, rhododendrons, and nightshades.

Advance to frame #15, miscellaneous.

In your own words . . .

> Our final category of poisons includes some more common killers of animals that we don't often think about. Chocolate is dangerous for dogs, and food poisoning from garbage is harmful to all animals.

Advance to frame #16, poison locations.

In your own words . . .

> Now that we have identified some of the poisons we need to be concerned about, let's look at the danger points in our homes that are most likely to present poison hazards.
>
> The most common poison locations are the kitchen, bathroom, garage, and everywhere else in your home. No place is totally safe.

Advance to frame #17, kitchens.

In your own words . . .

> The kitchen is a dangerous place. The fact that we eat and cook there seems to lessen our level of awareness to potential poisoning hazards. Look for ammonia, bleach, dish soap, drain cleaners, furniture polish, and cleaning powders.

Advance to frame #18, bathroom.

In your own words . . .

> Bathrooms are second nature to all of us. We seldom, if ever, think about the poisons we keep there. Almost all bathrooms have at least one serious poison hazard.
>
> Look for cleaning agents, cosmetics, deodorants, over-the-counter medications, prescription drugs, and rubbing alcohol.

Advance to frame #19, garage.

In your own words . . .

> Garages seem like the most common place for poisons, and they usually have a number sitting on shelves and on work benches.
>
> Antifreeze, fertilizer, gasoline, lighter fluids, paint, paint remover, paint thinner, pesticides, rat poisons, and weed killers are just part of the list of poisons our garages may contain.

Advance to frame #20, other places.

In your own words...

> While the other areas in our home are somewhat easier to recognize, the rest of the house still offers plenty of opportunities for poisons.
>
> Cigarettes, matches, plants, and paint chips are just some of the poisoning hazards appearing in almost every home.

Interaction—feedback level one—10 minutes

Advance to frame #21, making a list.

In your own words . . .

> Now that we have identified the types of poisons we might find in our homes and the places that we might find them, let's look room by room through a typical home and see what poisons we can find..

What room should we start with?

> **Work through each room in a typical house and list possible poisons in each room. Using a flip chart, begin to make lists for each room. You may want to ask for a volunteer to help write the lists on the flip charts. Be sure to offer obviously missing examples, but wait as long as possible for a learner to offer them first.**
>
> **Be sure to also look at the garage and yard.**

Interaction—feedback level two—10 minutes

Advance to frame #22, making a map.

In your own words . . .

> Now we are going to take poison prevention to your home. One of the most effective ways to spot poison trouble spots is by drawing a map of your house and identifying places where you need to be watchful for problems.
>
> On the paper provided, quickly draw a map of your home. If you have more than one floor you should just pick the floor likely to have the most hazards. You can later finish your map drawing all of your floors.
>
> Now pick a partner next to you and show the person your map. Look at your partner's map and have your partner look at yours. Offer

any comments to your partner about his or her map and have your partner comment on yours. Make sure that your partner has identified all the potential trouble spots. When you get home, use your map to check for poisons, and fix any problems you may have.

Circulate around the room and make sure everyone is following instructions. Assist those needing any help.

Interaction—feedback level three—5 minutes

In your own words . . .

If you have finished working with your partner, make any changes necessary to your map. If you have any questions, please let me know so that I can work with you.

Observe the participants and assist where necessary.

Evaluation—10 minutes

Advance to frame #23, volunteer.

In your own words . . .

I would like to have one of you show the group your map and describe your hazards.

After you have secured a volunteer, assist the volunteer making the presentation. Answer any questions the volunteer or other participants ask.

In your own words . . .

Make sure your map looks similar to this one and let me know if I can help you in any way. I will stay after the class and assist anyone who needs help. I don't want you to leave without a map that is going to work to prevent a poisoning in your home.

Thanks for volunteering.

Closure—5 minutes

Advance to frame #24, the poison center.

In your own words . . .

Before we quit, I want to give you some important information in the event you should face a possible poisoning situation.

First, here is the number for the local Poison Center: It is 202.625.3333.

Advance to frame #25, information.

In your own words . . .

Here is the information you will need when you call:

- age of patient
- condition of patient
- weight
- health history
- exact name of the product
- size of the container
- strength of the product
- when the poisoning occurred
- amount of the exposure
- personal contact information.

I hope you never have to call the Poison Center, but if you do, you will at least have a good idea of the information you will need to give.

This information is in your brochure that you will take home with you.

Advance to frame #26, good-bye.

In your own words . . .

Thanks for attending tonight and please take the time to fill out an evaluation sheet. You can just leave it by the door as you leave.

Be sure to use your maps to make your homes safe from possible poisoning hazards.

Good-bye!

Close the session and assist any participants with remaining questions. Be sure all participants have taken a brochure with them.

Resources

Following is a list of Websites that provide a variety of information on ISD, evaluation, and learning theory. These sites are from academic institutions, associations, and professionals who have expertise in one or more aspects of ISD.

ISD

http://www.nwlink.com/%7Edonclark/hrd/sat1.html. Big Dog's ISD Site.

http://www.seas.gwu.edu/~tlooms/ISD/isd_homepage.html. Instructional design methodologies and techniques.

http://infoweb.magi.com/~broadb/sat.html. A nine-step ISD model.

http://www.seas.gwu.edu/~sbraxton/ISD/instruction_models.html. ISD models based on learning theory.

http://www.gwu.edu/~tip/gagne.html. Gagne's nine events with Quicktime movie of Gagne.

http://www.wested.org/tie/dlrn/blooms.html. Bloom's taxonomy.

Theory and Evaluation

http://www.eval.org. American Evaluation Association.

http://www.coedu.usf.edu/inst_tech/resources/competen.html. List of competencies and skills by Analysis & Technology, Inc.

http://www.edtech.univnorthco.edu/disswww/dissdir.htm. Directory of doctoral dissertations in educational technology (1977-1999).

http://www.hs.nki.no/%7Emorten/cmcped.htm. Paper on pedagogical techniques for computer-mediated communication.

http://www.enable.evitech.fi/enable99/papers/sioutine/sioutine.html. Paper on project management of courseware systems for distance learning programs.

http://www.cudenver.edu/~mryder/itc_data/idmodels.html. University of Colorado instructional design and learning theory links.

http://www.gwu.edu/%7Etip/theories.html. Description of almost every learning theory.

http://www.gwu.edu/~tip/domains.html. Comprehensive list of learning domains.

http://www.ido.gmu.edu/instructionalmodels.asp. IRC's instructional resource links.

http://coe.sdsu.edu/eet/. Encyclopedia of Educational Technology.

Distance Education and Technology

http://itech1.coe.uga.edu/EPSS/EPSS.html. Electronic performance support systems (EPSS) resources.

http://www.unc.edu/courses/ssp/ped.html. Resources from the University of North Carolina-Chapel Hill, Center for Instructional Technology Pedagogical.

http://snow.utoronto.ca/best/crsreview.html. Best practices in Web-based instruction: Review of online courses.

http://www.wested.org/tie/dlrn/. The Distance Learning Resource Network, the dissemination project for the U.S. Department of Education Star Schools Program.

http://curry.edschool.Virginia.Edu/go/ITcases/home.html. Case studies in instructional technology and design from the Instructional Technology Program at the Curry School of Education, University of Virginia.

http://www.library.miami.edu/tools/tools.html. Teaching on the Web, the University of Miami's resources and tools.

http://web.missouri.edu/%7Ec709707/necc/. Analysis of student perceptions on distance learning.

http://www.wisc.edu/learntech/grp/id.htm. Learning technology and distance education links from the University of Wisconsin.

http://www.cudenver.edu/%7Emryder/itc_data/distance.html. Distance education links from the University of Colorado.

http://fcae.nova.edu/%7Eburmeist/idlinks.html. Links related to instructional design from Marsha Burmeister at Nova Southeastern University.

http://www.inform.umd.edu/TeachTech/design.html. Instructional design links from University of Maryland.

The Author

Chuck Hodell is the director of the Educational Design Unit of the George Meany Center for Labor Studies-National Labor College in Silver Spring, Maryland. He is also on the faculty at the University of Maryland Baltimore County (UMBC) in the graduate program in instructional systems development. Hodell has published numerous articles on educational design for ASTD. He is working on a Ph.D. in language, literacy, and culture from UMBC, where he also received his master's degree in instructional systems development. His undergraduate degree is from Antioch University—The George Meany Center in Labor Studies. He can be contacted at: 116 Swan Road, Stevensville, MD 21666; email: chuck@hodell.com.